BLOOMING IN BROKEN PLACES

The Journey to Abundant Life through Brokenness

Blessings!
2 Cor 1:4

DEBORAH MALONE

Deborah Malone

LAMP POST
publishers

OTHER BOOKS BY DEBORAH MALONE

Trixie Montgomery Cozy Mysteries
Death in Dahlonega
Murder in Marietta
Terror on Tybee Island
Chilled in Chattanooga

Skye Southerland Cozy Mystery Series
Buckhead Dead
Decatur Dead

BLOOMING IN BROKEN PLACES
by Deborah Malone

Published by:

LAMP POST
publishers
SPRING VALLEY · CALIFORNIA
www.lamppostpublishers.com

Trade Paperback: ISBN-13 # 978-1-60039-239-9
ebook: ISBN-13 # 978-1-60039-744-8

Contents

Foreword

I'm so glad that you've chosen *Blooming in Broken Places!* I thought about you just this morning. No really, I did! As I picked the flower growing in my concrete steps, I thought about the ladies all over the country who will be encouraged by Debbie's wonderful book, and I said a prayer for you.

You're facing challenges – either present ones that cause you to wither or one that happened long ago that still makes you wilt when you think about them. And you're wondering how you can thrive with so much negativity that seems to suck the life out of you. You can relate to the broken places Debbie talks about. Broken dreams, broken promises, broken marriages. But there's hope! I know because I've been there.

Filled with upbeat stories about ladies from the Bible and Debbie's own intriguing story of overcoming obstacles and flourishing because of her faith, *Blooming in Broken Places* will rejuvenate your spirit and inspire you to draw closer to Jesus and let him resuscitate your soul.

You can tell by the chapter titles that this book is right for you. Here are a few of them: Keep on Blooming – Even When Overwhelmed; Keep on Blooming – Even When You've Made a Huge Mistake; Keep on Blooming – Even When Your Circumstances Are Not What You Want Them to Be.

Perfect for individual study or small groups, *Blooming in Broken Places* offers "A Verse to Bloom By," "A Prayer to Bloom By" and Application Questions at the end of each of the twelve chapters that help you apply biblical principles Debbie shares.

So go on! Get started! Learn how to bloom – even in broken places!

Julie Morris
Author of *Guided By Him...to a Thinner, Not so Stressed-Out You!*
www.guidedbyhim.com

Preface

Over the years many people have asked me to write my story. It just wasn't the right time. Last year when I was writing the third book in the *Skye Southerland Cozy Mystery Series,* I was led to write *Blooming in Broken Places.*

Even though my life's had some gritty moments, I wanted the book to be encouraging, so I came up with the idea of weaving my story with those of women from the Bible who God used even when they were in their darkest places. After researching, I came away full of encouragement and feeling blessed. I discovered that God frequently used broken women for his glory.

Another thing I have learned through the trials I've endured is that God's timing is not always our timing. Just because our goals or dreams haven't been realized doesn't mean they won't be. We might have to wait longer than expected, but during that time God can and will use us.

I hope that my story, as well as the stories of Miriam, Esther, Rahab and others, will encourage you and fill you with hope. My one wish is that you will learn that you, too, can bloom in your broken places.

One more thought before you begin:

As I share my own personal stories and experiences through the coming pages, I touch upon the lives of many people (whose names have been changed) who have been a part of my own journey, who have affected it both positively and negatively. But my focus is not to share how wrongly I was treated or to present to you the uglier side of any particular individual — this story is not about them; nor is it to garner empathy for my struggles or spark your ire for my sake — this story is not about me. Rather, this story is about how God can use the darkest times of our lives to help us recognize His presence as we walk through the valley of the shadow of death, to aid us in rising above our fears, and to cause us to bloom in our broken places.

This story is about Him.

And Him alone.

Deborah Malone

Acknowledgments

When I first decided to write my story, I sent out the call for a co-author. I received many replies, but was drawn to fellow author Julie Morris. When I went to meet with her, she surprised me by saying that she would mentor me, but did not want to take part in the writing. She said, "This is your baby." At first I was discouraged, but the more I wrote, the more I understood what she was talking about. It was something only I could write. Julie helped with editing, and contributed her thoughts to *Blooming in Broken Places*. Julie, thank you for encouraging me to finish something I didn't think I could do.

I want to thank my family and friends for standing behind me and encouraging me to write *Blooming in Broken Places*.

As always, a special thanks to my editor, Beverly Nault.

*Mother, my brother Lee, me, and my brother Lewis,
with Great-Grandmother in the back.*

BLOOMING
IN
BROKEN
PLACES

CHAPTER ONE

KEEP ON BLOOMING

Even When Overwhelmed

Listen! Can you hear Jochebed calling?

"Miriam, Miriam, where are you?" Jochebed frantically pleaded. "I want you to hide in the reeds and make sure Moses is safe. Come and report back to me."

> *About this time, a man and a woman from the tribe of Levi got married. The woman became pregnant and gave birth to a son. She saw that he was a special baby and kept him hidden for three months. But when she could no longer hide him, she got a basket made of papyrus and waterproofed it with tar and pitch. She put the baby in the basket and laid it among the reeds along the bank of the Nile River. The baby's sister then stood at a distance, watching to see what would happen to him.*
>
> *Exodus 2:1-4*

Wow! Talk about putting responsibility on a child's shoulders. I don't know why Jochebed, Moses' mother, asked such a great task of young Miriam.

Maybe she thought Miriam, being a child, could hide in the reeds easier than she could, a grown woman. For whatever reason, Miriam was chosen to keep watch on her baby brother.

I can only imagine how scared she must have been, but she didn't want to let her mother down.

The night songs of the cicadas and the sweet breeze caressing my skin lulled me to sleep. The memories of visiting my Aunt Maudie's house are sweet and dear. But all my memories aren't so sweet.

I looked like any other little girl my age – carefree and without a worry in the world. But at six years old I carried the weight of the world on my shoulders.

Fear and uncertainty had taken up residence inside my head and haunted me regularly. Every morning when it was time to get ready for school my constant companions would rear their ugly heads whispering, *Your mother will fall while you're gone, or she'll be in the hospital when you get back. Then what? After all it's your responsibility to make sure she's safe.*

What I couldn't express in words at such a young age came out as screaming, stomping my feet and rolling around on the floor. Because Mother wasn't physically able to take me to school, I'm sure I thought that would convince her to keep me home. It didn't. She just called Dad and he'd come home from work and take me. This happened several times, until one day our principal, Mr. Lane, met Dad at my first-grade classroom door. "Sir, you go on back to work and I'll take care of this."

Now Dad was a big man, but Mr. Lane was bigger, and he always had a round, fat cigar sticking out of his mouth. It only took one spanking from Mr. Lane to convince me it was in my best interest to get on the school bus. The monsters taunting me about mother's health would get to stay home – the place I wished I could be to prevent her from dying while I was learning to read. Even though I couldn't help her, of course I wanted to be with her.

Once, my mother's mother was visiting from Miami and I thought I could get her on my side. Grandma was as big around as she was tall, and she'd been a charge nurse for many years. She didn't take any guff from others – and she sure wasn't taking it from me.

The sun was already high in the sky, and it promised to be a great day to stay home and visit with Grandma. After my two brothers boarded the bus, I happily informed her I was staying home that day. She didn't like my idea one bit. Right there in front of God and all the other kids on the bus, she pulled up my dress and wore out my little hiney. I got on the bus with tears streaming down my cheeks. I don't know which was more painful that day, the actual spanking or the humiliation. Now don't get me wrong, I loved Grandma dearly, which made it hurt all the worse.

There was a reason I bucked going to school. Mother's body was riddled with Rheumatoid Arthritis. At the age of twelve she was diagnosed with Still's Disease, the name given childhood arthritis. Suffice it to say, she didn't have an easy childhood.

Mother was born and raised in Cincinnati, Ohio, with her two younger brothers. When she got sick, the doctors were baffled and couldn't come up with a diagnosis. Bedridden, she experienced high fevers, lost all her hair and was racked with pain. It took months for a concrete diagnosis, and she remained in bed for two years before the hideous disease went into remission.

Grandma and Granddad divorced when my mother was young. I don't remember my granddad at all. I've seen pictures of him holding my brothers when they were babies. He was as tall and skinny as my grandma was round. He left Grandma with three small children to raise and married his cousin.

Mother and her two brothers were raised by Grandma and my great-grandmother. Grandma worked full-time while raising her three children. Oddly enough, it was my granddad's mother who helped raise Mother and her siblings.

I remember going to visit relatives in Cincinnati; we'd pile in our old station wagon, strap the luggage rack on top and head up north. Dad would put the seats down and Mother would lie on a mattress in the back. Never mind seat belts in those days. The cars didn't even have them.

Great-grandmother lived in an apartment building, an oddity to be sure. Growing up in the country I didn't see many high-rise apartments. With gray hair and a kind face, she always appeared old to me. She was as sweet as molasses and always glad to see us. I love the pictures I have of us kids at her house. Many a time I sat on the stairs to the upstairs apartments and bumped down them one at a time.

I can't say her daughter, my Great-Aunt Grumpy, inherited her disposition. Of course that's not her real name, but it sure does describe her right nicely. With a chiseled face and a sharp nose, she reminded me a little of the witch in the *Wizard of Oz*. I had the sense even back then she didn't like children too much. As far as I know, she never married and always lived with Great-Grandma.

Mother lived in Cincinnati when my parents met. She was twenty-one and Dad was thirty-three. Dad grew up in Opelika, Alabama, and had moved to Cincinnati to work at General Electric. Talk about a fish out of water – country boy meets big city girl.

Tall and dark, Dad cut a handsome figure of a man – one to be reckoned with at well over six feet tall. Just his size and demeanor were enough to strike fear into any foe. Dad owned a 1948 Indian motorcycle which he and Mother rode on dates. It wasn't unusual for Dad to ride it back and forth between Alabama and Cincinnati. They married shortly after they met and began their family. My two older brothers were born in Cincinnati.

They lived in a two-story house which they bought from Grandma. They would later sell it to Mother's brother, and that is where he raised his family until the 1970s. The house still stands and I like to drive by it when I visit. My brothers, Lee and Lewis, were four and five years older than me. They lived in the house for several years before they moved south.

When the boys weren't much older than toddlers, they locked Mother out of the house and went up to the second floor, hung out the window and waved cheerfully to her.

When Mother married Dad, she'd been in remission. Having children caused the arthritis to rear its ugly head again. While the boys were young her joints began to deteriorate. In 1953, she and Dad packed up my brothers and transferred to Georgia where Dad worked at the newly opened General

Electric Plant. Even though it was a sacrifice on Mother's part, it was a win-win situation for Dad. He found much-needed work closer to home.

It amazes me that Mother left her family, and especially her doctors, to move to a little town in north Georgia. I don't think I'd have been able to make such a move. Not only did she have my two rambunctious brothers to deal with, but in 1954, her sweet little girl was born. Well, I don't know how sweet I was, but that's a perk in being the author of a book. You get to write it like you want.

Having three children had taken a terrible toll on Mother's health and body. Her hips and knees had frozen in 90-degree angles. When she stood, her legs remained in a sitting position. Her toes and fingers, ravished by this terrible disease, were twisted sideways. She was no longer able to stand on her own – she had to use crutches, or a wheelchair. Hospital stays were the norm for Mother and this was when we would either stay by ourselves, while Dad went and checked on her, or we would stay with someone my parents knew. I remember, on more than one occasion, staying with people I didn't know and wondering if Dad would come back and pick us up. So you can imagine how hard it was for me to leave mother and go off to school, wondering if she'd be at home or back in the hospital when I got off the bus that afternoon.

From the outside, our family seemed normal, and just like everyone else's in our suburban neighborhood. We lived in a nice wood-framed house just outside the city limits. The house sat on a hill with a big field at the bottom where we'd play baseball and other sports with the neighborhood kids. I have memories living there that are as sweet as the succulent red rose bushes that stood sentry between the side of the house and the woods. But life wasn't always rosy.

Inside the little house on the hill, storms brewed frequently. Dad had a temper as big as he was. Even though Mother was disabled there were times Dad hit her. I remember Mother taking us kids in the middle of the night to her friend's house and when she opened the door I blurted through tears, "Daddy hit Mother again." The image of us standing in that doorway still haunts me.

Eventually, as we children got older and were able to take on some responsibility, the physical abuse stopped, but the turmoil never did. We all carry scars from our childhood, and Dad was no different. He had scars of his own.

It wasn't easy being the only girl in the neighborhood at the time. One time the boys convinced me they were doing me a grand favor by letting me pitch. Tomboy that I was, I took them up on it, and they kept batting with all their might. I handled their hits fairly well until Darin, one of the Fletcher boys, hit me in the shoulder with a line drive. I couldn't move my shoulder for over a week and it turned the prettiest shades of blue and green. I wore that bruise like a badge of honor and drug every bit of sympathy I could get out of anyone who'd take a look. I didn't go to the emergency room. After all, it was just a bruise, Dad said. It wasn't until a few years ago, after a shoulder injury and x-rays, my doctor told me I'd once broken my collar bone. I knew exactly when it happened.

Life back then was filled with childhood injuries. Back in the day you didn't wear shoes in the summer. I don't know exactly what happened, but I must have stepped into a yellow jacket nest one day. Both feet were stung so bad they swelled until I was unable to walk, ran a fever and threw up – I didn't go to the emergency room that time either. I really can't blame Dad, he was probably sick of taking Mother to the hospital, and our childhood injuries were minor in comparison to her pain.

Then there was the time I was a toddler and my brothers put the car in neutral and it rolled down our steep driveway with the door open. We lived surrounded by woods, and I remember another time coming down the hill from the Fletcher's when Lee, Lewis and I were chased by a black racer snake.

None of my injuries were ever life-threatening, unlike my bother Lewis. It was one of the many times when Mother was in the hospital that we had an actual baby sitter. She had taken us into the woods for a picnic. Lewis decided to see how high he could climb up a pine tree when a branch broke. As he fell downwards the broken part tore into the flesh of his upper arm. This happened the same time Dad was bringing Mother home from another stay in the hospital. He got Mother inside, turned around and took Lewis to get his arm sewn up. He had stitches inside his arm from his armpit to his elbow.

Dad obviously missed the country life, because he kept buying farm animals. He owned a few acres of land – not nearly enough for farming. That didn't deter Dad. He built a chicken coop in our back yard to raise chickens. It was kind of hard playing with a chicken one day and eating it the next.

When we were younger, Callie came several days a week to help with chores around the house. There were many days, I remember, when Callie took a chicken and wrung its neck, and then we'd have fried chicken for supper. She possessed the most beautiful mahogany skin and she'd listen to me as long as I had something to say.

Then there was the time Dad bought a hog (and I don't mean a cute little piglet). This hog was downright mean and dangerous. The escape artist kept getting out and wreaking havoc at the neighbor's house. Dad would have to leave work and come home to catch the errant hog. This happened half a dozen times before Dad had enough of the persistent hog's shenanigans. Boy, that was some of the best bacon and ham I've ever eaten. I'm sure Dad thought so too.

Let's don't forget the donkey. What was Grandma thinking? How she ended up with a donkey I still don't know, but she needed to get rid of it. So, what does one do with a donkey in Miami? Why, give it to your son-in-law in Georgia, of course. Dad drove down in the family car, took the back seat out, and loaded the donkey for a ride back to Georgia. Dad got more mileage out of that story. He'd tell how the donkey laid his head on Dad's shoulder and the looks this odd picture garnered from passers-by.

It turned out a donkey doesn't make a good pet for three young children. Who does Dad, in turn, sell the donkey to? The milkman, who else? Saturday rolled around and he came in his milk truck to pick up our friend. We waved as the truck disappeared down the driveway.

Mother supervised and kept up with her active family as much as she could, even as her illness waxed and waned. I believe Mother's strong faith helped her through her toughest times.

When the princess saw the basket among the reeds, she sent her maid to get it for her. When the princess opened it, she saw the baby. The little boy was crying, and she felt sorry for him. "This must be one of the Hebrew children," she said.

Exodus 2:5-6

We can only wonder how Miriam felt. Was she scared? If so, despite her fear, she stayed until she saw the Pharaoh's daughter bathe in the Nile and discover the baby. Gazing into the basket at the crying child, she exclaimed, "This must be a Hebrew baby."

The baby's sister approached the princess. "Should I go and find one of the Hebrew women to nurse the baby for you?" she asked.

Exodus 2:7

Miriam saw her chance and jumped on the opportunity to reunite Moses with his mother. She bravely approached the Princess and asked, "Should I go and find one of the Hebrew women to nurse the baby for you?"

"Yes, do!" the Princess replied.

Miriam ran breathlessly to get her mother and bring her back to the Nile. She pulled on her mother's arm, "Come Mother, come quickly, something wonderful has happened." The Princess allowed Jochebed to nurse Moses until he was old enough to be weaned. Then she returned him to the palace, as an Egyptian.

Miriam, Moses and their brother Aaron grew into adulthood. Because of her early experience of being Moses' protector, I often wonder if Miriam felt responsible for Moses. After all, she was his big sister. From my own experiences, I believe she did.

Many years later, when Moses had grown up, he went out to visit his own people, the Hebrews, and he saw how hard they were forced to work. During his visit, he saw an Egyptian beating one of his fellow Hebrews. After looking in all directions to make sure no one was watching, Moses killed the Egyptian and hid the body in the sand.
Exodus 2:11-12

Moses was raised in the palace as an Egyptian, but he felt a kinship with the Hebrews. One day while visiting his people, he saw an Egyptian beating a fellow Hebrew. He looked around to make sure no one was watching, killed the Egyptian and buried him in the sand. Moses thought he'd done a bang-up job until the next day when he returned to the area and saw two Hebrews fighting. He asked one of them, "Why are you beating up your friend?"

The fellow was a little more than perturbed that Moses had interrupted their fight. "Who appointed you prince and judge?" Very like our present day saying, "Who made you judge and jury?"

Oops! Moses messed up. The cat was out of the bag and he knew before long word would spread he'd killed an Egyptian.

And sure enough Pharaoh heard what had happened, and he tried to kill Moses. But Moses fled from Pharaoh and went to live in the land of Midian.
Exodus 2:15

Fearing for his life, he fled to Midian. While drawing water from one of the local wells, he rescued some women being harassed by a bunch of hooligans. Their father was so grateful he gave Moses his daughter, Zipporah, to marry. Moses married her, even though she was a foreigner.

One day Moses was tending the flock of his father-in-law, Jethro, the priest of Midian. He led the flock far into the wilderness and came to Sinai, the mountain of God. There the angel of the Lord appeared to him in a blazing fire from the middle of a bush. Moses stared in amazement. Though the bush was engulfed in flames, it didn't burn up. "This is amazing," Moses said to himself. "Why isn't that bush burning up? I must go see it."

When the Lord saw Moses coming to take a closer look, God called to him from the middle of the bush, "Moses, Moses!"

"Here I am!" Moses replied.

Exodus 3:1-4

Sometime after Moses married, he met God in the burning bush. I could relate to Moses, who didn't feel qualified to be God's spokesperson. God told Moses he was going to lead his people out of bondage. You'd think hearing a booming voice emanating from a burning bush would be enough to scare anyone into submission. But not Moses. He felt he wasn't good enough to speak to the Pharaoh on behalf of his people. "Why me, Lord? Surely you've made a mistake." What? Moses just told God he made a mistake? Did he have a death wish?

"No, I don't think so Moses. Don't worry, I'll be there with you." How many times in the Bible are we told that God will always be with us, but we continue to hold onto our fears?

God finally told Moses he'd give him signs to use. First, he'd be able to turn his staff into a snake. Surely this would be enough to convince Moses to hightail it to the Pharaoh carrying God's message. But Moses held on to his fear like a security blanket instead of giving it over to God. "O Lord, I'm not very good with words. I never have been, and I'm not now, even though you have spoken to me. I get tongue-tied, and my words get tangled." Wow! Have you ever felt that way?

Then the Lord became angry with Moses. "All right," he said. "What about your brother, Aaron the Levite? I know he speaks well. And look! He is on his way to meet you now. He will be delighted to see you. Talk to him, and put the words in his mouth. I will be with both of you as you speak, and I will instruct you both in what to do. Aaron will be your spokesman to the people.

Exodus 4:14-16

Finally, Moses resorted to begging, "Lord, please! Send anyone else." Doesn't sound much like a leader, does he? But God saw something in Moses he didn't see in himself. God took someone who wanted no part of his plan and used him! Right where he was - fear and all. You could say he brought Moses into this job kicking and screaming.

God decided he'd give Moses a shot of confidence by sending his brother Aaron to be his mouthpiece. He'd give Moses the words and Aaron would speak them. It took the Pharaoh a little while, but after several plagues, he finally got the message and let the Hebrews go.

Then Miriam the prophet, Aaron's sister, took a tambourine and led all the women as they played their tambourines and danced. And Miriam sang this song: "Sing to the Lord, for he has triumphed gloriously; he has hurled both horse and rider into the red sea."

Exodus 15:20-21

Miriam and Moses reunited while they were on their wilderness journey. God had appointed Miriam a prophetess, which meant she was a messenger of God and spoke in his name. God had blessed her with a holy gift. Miriam was an inspiration to her people, especially the women. She would make music with her tambourine and sing a song of praise, "Sing to the Lord, for he has triumphed gloriously; horse and rider he has thrown into the sea."

Miriam had accomplished much in her life. She'd shown how heroic she was watching out for Moses, shown strong leadership to the other women in the wilderness and shown great faith in God. This proves God used only perfect women, right? Well, no, not exactly.

That's not the end of Miriam's story. We find out she's just like the rest of us – human, with human emotions.

While they were at Hazeroth, Miriam and Aaron criticized Moses because he had married a Cushite woman. They said, "Has the Lord spoken only through Moses? Hasn't he spoken through us, too?"

Numbers 12:1-2

Miriam and Aaron had never approved of Moses' wife. The Israelites looked down on marrying a foreigner, especially those who worshiped idols. It was a normal reaction for Miriam and Aaron to disapprove of Moses' choice of a wife. But this most likely led to strife between brother and sister.

Even though she strove to please God, Miriam fell short. She and Aaron had important positions – Miriam was a great leader of the women – but they didn't possess the authority given to Moses. Remember, Miriam had been Moses' protector and big sister. Now he was getting all the attention. She envied that attention and the authority Moses held. So what did she do about it? She responded like any other human when frustrated – she complained to anyone who'd listen. But God was listening, too.

> But the Lord heard them. So immediately the Lord called to Moses, Aaron, and Miriam and said, "Go out to the Tabernacle, all three of you!" So the three of them went to the Tabernacle.
>
> *Numbers 12:2,4*

Oops! Not a good idea to complain about God's most trusted spokesperson. The Lord was not pleased. Kind of reminds me of when my parents used my middle name – "Deborah Jean!"

God appeared in a cloud and confronted Aaron and Miriam. He basically asked who they thought they were to criticize his servant Moses? He was so angry at Miriam that he struck her with a case of leprosy. Immediately, the crowd shunned her.

Moses could have used this as a gotcha moment, but he chose the high road. He didn't take pleasure in her pain, or gloat in God's chastisement. Instead, he begged God to heal Miriam. After seven days, God did heal her and she was reunited with her people. Though she had been punished, her people still held her in high regard.

So Miriam was kept outside the camp for seven days, and the people waited until she was brought back before they traveled again.

Numbers 12:15

Tradition tells us that after her death her funeral was celebrated in the most solemn manner for thirty days. Like her brothers Aaron and Moses, Miriam did not reach the Promised Land but died in the wilderness; however, her cry of exultation, "Sing unto the Lord," which had signified freedom for the newborn Israel, could not die.

All the Women of the Bible

Bless Miriam's pea-picking heart. Even though this great woman of influence loved God and strove to please him, her human side prevailed.

Let's take one last look at Miriam's life. Did God wait until she was "perfect" to use her to teach and lead his people? No, he didn't. He used Miriam right where she was in her life, flaws and all. Can God use us, flaws and all? You betcha!

I think Miriam and I would have a lot to talk about. I can picture us sitting on a porch swing, sipping some good ole sweet tea, maybe eating a 'mater biscuit, comparing the responsibilities we had as children.

A thought to bloom by

Miriam was overwhelmed with responsibilities – greater than she should have been for her age.

A verse to bloom by

I can do everything through Christ, who gives me strength.

Philippians 4:13

A prayer to bloom by

Abba, I come to you with praise on my lips thanking you for everything you have given me; even the very air I breathe. Abba, sometimes I get overwhelmed with all the responsibilities I have. Please give me the strength to handle these responsibilities and thank you for never leaving me to handle these tasks alone. In Jesus' name, amen.

APPLICATION QUESTIONS:

· Have you ever been overwhelmed with responsibilities?

· What happened?

CHAPTER TWO

KEEP ON BLOOMING

Even When You've Made a Mistake

"The devil made me do it!" Poor Evie. She earned the distinction of committing the original sin, and bless her heart, she hasn't lived it down yet. I believe God gives us warnings in the form of a nudge or gut feeling. But in Eve's circumstance, she was told outright by her Father not to eat the fruit of the Tree of Knowledge.

> *The Lord God placed the man in the Garden of Eden to tend and watch over it. But the Lord God warned him, "You may freely eat the fruit of every tree in the garden – except the tree of the knowledge of good and evil. If you eat this fruit, you are sure to die."*
>
> *Genesis 2:15-17*

Eve wasn't the only one who didn't heed God's warning.

When I was in the third grade, my parents built a house next door to the one I'd grown up in. We moved into the new house when I was eight years old.

Mother depended on me from an early age to help take care of her personal needs. Over the years, I became her caregiver in every way. I dressed her every morning before leaving for school. I helped her with her hygiene. I clipped her toenails, changed bandages on open wounds and just about anything she needed done.

As soon as I was old enough to reach the stove, I came in from school and cooked supper. On weekends, I cleaned house. On more than one occasion Mother came and picked me up at a friend's house first thing on a Saturday morning so I could get an early start on cleaning. If it wasn't done right, I had to do it over. I learned I could get away with it sometimes by saying, "Mother, didn't I do a great job?" That didn't happen too often after she caught on. Our house was a virtual showcase. She made sure the outside looked as good as the inside. She literally lived her life through me.

Reading was my escape from reality and it helped take away some of the emotional pain. My love of reading started early. I wouldn't be surprised if I'd come out of the womb holding a book. My appetite for books was insatiable.

I remember the wonderful scent, wafting through the air, in our little elementary school library. I'm not sure what it was – maybe dust, mold or just old books, but I loved that smell. It was comforting to me. My friend, Diane, introduced me to the downtown library and I was in book heaven. I know I read every young adult mystery on the shelves.

Many times I took a book, curled up on the top basement step, and read until Mother called me. Saturday mornings I'd get out of bed before anyone else, snuggle in front of the fireplace, and cozy up with a book before I had to put it down to clean the house. Books were my friends. They never asked anything of me or told me to rescrub the toilets or refold the laundry to their liking.

To my brothers' credit, they had responsibilities, too, but they were out of the house by the time I was in high school.

After they left, I assumed more duties. I soon took on outdoor chores as well. I mowed the grass, trimmed the bushes and dug up weeds.

Dad bought a riding lawn-mower that looked like a miniature tractor. That orange and black baby boasted five forwards and two reverses. I'd put that thing in fifth gear and have the lawn done in no time. I guess Mother didn't trust me with that much power because one day I came home to discover a Snapper mower sitting in the place of my tractor. It was a big disappointment, not to mention it took longer to mow the grass.

After we moved, Dad took a second job to support the family, and was rarely home. I'd be lying if I said I didn't resent the responsibilities. Many times, I missed out on school activities or other things kids my age were doing to meet my mother's expectations.

Anger wasn't the only foe that tormented me. Fear still dogged me like a hound on a coon's trail. Not only did I feel responsible for Mother's safety, I carried the worries of an adult. After all, I was thrown into adult situations early on. Even as a pre-teen, I'd make the grocery list, then Mother would drive us to the store and she'd sign a check. While she sat in the car, I'd go in, shop for groceries, check out and then fill in the amount on the check. I wonder if she had any idea the angst I felt during those trips.

Once, when we were at the store, I came out to find a young black woman sitting on the passenger side with the car door open. Blood ran down her legs. I panicked! I just knew Mother had hit this poor lady with the car and they were going to arrest her. It turned out the young woman was having a miscarriage and had asked Mother if she could sit down until help came.

When I was in middle school I played basketball and softball. Mother made a deal with my basketball coach to let her pick me up early from practice so I could go home and cook. Not once do I remember my parents coming to a game. I know Mother wasn't able, but I never understood why Dad didn't come. It still tugs at my heart to know they never saw me play sports.

We lived in a beautiful brick home and lacked for nothing. Except for one thing – peace. It would have been hard enough if we'd had good family dynamics. But that wasn't the case. Dad was a strong-willed man, to put it nicely. I regret not talking to his younger sister before she died to find out more about his childhood. I'll never fully understand the demons he lived with all his life, and what caused him to treat us the way he did.

I know when he was four, his biological mother died and his father married a woman younger than his older sister, which must have caused unusual family dynamics.

Dad spent most of his growing-up years on the farm, and like many children of his time, only went to the eighth grade before leaving school to work in the fields. It was a hard life to say the least. Despite having little formal education, Dad managed to provide well for his family. But his strong will and temper shadowed him all his life.

Aunt Maudie, his older sister, was the closest thing to a grandmother on Dad's side. I loved her dearly. Dad moved in with her when he was a teenager and he lived with her until he left home. I loved going to her house in Alabama. It was a time when the atmosphere would be peaceful between my parents and I wasn't expected to do anything but be a child. My brothers and I would climb the old mimosa tree in the back yard and play until it was dark.

The sweet aroma of homemade biscuits and adult talk wafting from the kitchen woke me up to a big breakfast of eggs, bacon and pear preserves Aunt Maudie had put up. She could turn anything you could grow in a garden or raise on a farm into an unforgettable meal. She possessed the gentlest spirit of any woman I'd ever met.

One of her sons was a master carpenter and helped build two houses for Dad. It broke my heart when I was old enough to understand he was an alcoholic. Although, in time I made a game out of seeing how many bottles of liquor I could find that he'd hidden in Aunt Maudie's house.

When we visited Aunt Maudie's, we'd go over to the boarding house where he lived, pick him up, and bring him back to her house for a visit. I loved being around him when he was sober. Eventually, he fell down the steps at the boarding house, broke his neck and died.

Dad was a godly man, and I have no doubt he loved his family. He and Mother made sure we attended church every time the doors opened. That early background in church became a building block for my faith. But Dad's high expectations of us kids and our church's rigid beliefs set the bar high. I received many a bloody nose trying to reach that bar. I remember when I was probably five or six, standing in the yard, looking up in the sky crying out to God to forgive me. I don't remember what I did, but it must have been a doozy. It would be many years before I truly knew and understood God's grace.

Dad had to have been over-whelmed at times. Working two jobs, taking care of three small children, and having the responsibility of a sick wife was a tremendous burden. These life circumstances opened the gates for discord in our family.

I woke up and went to bed listening to my parents argue. I vowed my marriage would be different. It wasn't!

I met my husband when I was nineteen, fell head over heels in love and was married in three months. Nineteen is way too young to be married, but you couldn't have convinced me. After all, what did my parents know about a happy marriage?

I thought he was the most handsome man I'd ever seen. He worked in law enforcement and was a striking figure in his uniform. He worked security where I attended junior college. I remember when he called and asked me for a date I ran through the house whooping, yelling and jumping on the bed. Doesn't sound much like someone who is mature enough to get married.

I believe, subconsciously, I thought this would relieve me of the tremendous pressure I felt at home. Little did I know I had jumped from the frying pan into the fire. I continued to be responsible for Mother, but now I had a husband who brought his own needs with him. I wish I could go back and tell that nineteen-year-old Debbie that three months is not enough time to know someone. Knowing myself at that vulnerable time, I probably wouldn't have listened anyway.

Between his baggage and mine, it made for a very dysfunctional family unit. I can't say that God didn't give me fair warning, though. There were times during our whirlwind relationship I had the gut feeling something wasn't right. How many times do we get that feeling, which I believe is the Holy Spirit's way of telling us to slow down and take a second look, but we ignore it? In my defense, I was still in my teens and had little experience in life-changing decisions. Maybe God should have whopped me up side my thick head instead of giving me a gentle nudge.

So God created human beings in his own image. In the image of God he created them; male and female he created them.

Genesis 1:27

From the beginning God created Adam and Eve equal in his sight. She was made from Adam's rib, next to his heart - not from a metatarsal foot bone for her to be tromped on.

God plainly said he created *them*, male and female, in his image. Knowing God considers us equal in his sight should empower all women. God chose to use women throughout the bible to further his message - and he didn't wait until they were perfect to use them. Eve, the mother of us all, was far from perfect.

The serpent was the shrewdest of all the wild animals the Lord God had made. One day he asked the woman, "Did

God really say you must not eat the fruit from any of the trees in the garden?"

Genesis 3:1

In his sly way, the serpent asked Eve a question he already knew the answer to, trying to make her think she had been slighted by God.

Did God really say you must not eat the fruit from any of the trees in the garden?

Genesis 3:1

At this point Eve answered with confidence. "Of course, we may eat fruit from the trees in the garden," the woman replied. "It's only the fruit from the tree in the middle of the garden that we are not allowed to eat. God said, 'You must not eat it or even touch it; if you do, you will die.'" In Genesis 3:2-3, God warned Eve and Adam not to eat of the fruit. He even told them they would die.

But the serpent wasn't about to give up, so he lied to her. *"'You won't die!' the serpent replied to the woman. 'God knows that your eyes will be opened as soon as you eat it, and you will be like God, knowing both good and evil'"* (Genesis 3:4-5). Well, he got that right! They learned about good and evil the hard way. And humans have been learning the hard way ever since.

The woman was convinced. She saw the tree was beautiful and its fruit looked delicious, and she wanted the wisdom it would give her. So she took some of the fruit and ate it. Then she gave some to her husband, who was with her, and he ate it, too. At that moment their eyes were opened, and they suddenly felt shame at their nakedness. So they sewed fig leaves together to cover themselves.

Genesis 3:6-7

The tree was beautiful and the fruit delighted her eyes. So, she took a bite and then gave Adam a bite. They messed up big time. As soon as they ate the fruit they realized they were naked. So, what did they do? They hid from God – or in their great wisdom they had gained from eating the fruit – they thought they could hide from God.

Of course, in this game of hide-and-seek it didn't take God long to find them.

When the cool evening breezes were blowing, the man and his wife heard the Lord God walking about in the garden. So they hid from the Lord God among the trees. Then the Lord God called to the man, "Where are you?"

He replied. "I heard you walking in the garden, so I hid. I was afraid because I was naked."

"Who told you that you were naked?" the Lord God asked. "Have you eaten from the tree whose fruit I commanded you not to eat?"

The man replied, "It was the woman you gave me who gave me the fruit, and I ate it."

Then the Lord God asked the woman, "What have you done?"

"The serpent deceived me," she replied. "That's why I ate it."

Genesis 3:8-13

Then the blame game started. Adam said Eve gave him the fruit and Eve said the serpent deceived her. God wasn't having any of it. This reminds me of my niece's son who had taken a magic marker and used the walls for a canvas. She asked him if he had done the dirty deed and he answered, "I didn't do it, Mama," while he held the tell-tale marker in his hand.

Just as we discipline our children when they've disobeyed, God disciplined his children. He told Eve, *"I will sharpen the pain of your pregnancy, and in your pain you will give birth..."* (Genesis 3:16). Having two children, I can attest to the fact he held up his end of the bargain.

Ladies, don't feel too bad for Eve, Adam got his comeuppance too. He would toil the earth the rest of his life, and he was banished from the gardens. Adam and Eve went on to have two sons, Cain and Abel.

> *When they grew up, Abel became a shepherd, while Cain cultivated the ground. When it was time for the harvest Cain presented some of his crops as a gift to the Lord. Abel also brought a gift – the best of the firstborn lambs from his flock. The Lord accepted Abel and his gift, but he did not accept Cain and his gift. This made Cain very angry, and he looked dejected.*
>
> *Genesis 4:2-5*

Now begins the real heartache. They've become a family unit, along with all the drama that comes with it. The boys grew into adults, and one day went to offer sacrifices to the Lord. Abel brought the best lamb from his flock. Cain brought produce from his garden that had already begun to rot. The

Lord found Cain's sacrifice unacceptable – this made Cain an unhappy camper.

> One day Cain suggested to his brother, "Let's go out into the fields." And while they were in the field, Cain attacked his brother, Abel, and killed him.
>
> Afterward the Lord said, "Where is your brother? Where is Abel?"
>
> "I don't know," Cain responded. "Am I my brother's guardian?"
>
> But the Lord said, "What have you done? Listen! Your brother's blood cries out to me from the ground! Now you are cursed and banished from the ground, which has swallowed your brother's blood. No longer will the ground yield good crops for you, no matter how hard you work! From now on you will be a homeless wanderer on the earth."
>
> Genesis 4:8-12

From this incident came the first murder. "Come on Abel, I've got something I want to show you." Cain enticed Abel into the field where he killed him. Even today, ironically, most murders are committed by family members. God punished Cain by banishing him from the region.

Eve is now feeling the full consequences of sin. Not only did she lose one of her sons to death, but she also lost Cain. She must live with the knowledge that Cain murdered Abel and that she would most likely never see Cain again.

This must have been the darkest point in her life. She had just lost both her sons. She might have asked herself if there was a reason to live. But after the darkness comes the light. She made it through the dark times, and the Bible never mentions her sinning again. Even though she was the first woman, who was far from perfect, we can see God working in her life.

> A long interval elapsed. Adam, we are told, was 130 years old when Eve gave birth to Seth, his name meaning "to appoint" or "to establish." And she took new courage in the fact, we know, for she said, "God hath appointed me another seed instead of Abel, whom Cain slew." A great seed this was to be, for the ancestry of Jesus Christ was to be traced back to the line of Seth.
>
> All the Women of the Bible

Sure, there's going to be times we mess up. There will even be times when God gives us a warning we don't heed, such as the negative feelings I had about my young marriage. But that doesn't mean we're alone in those dark times. We're told in Hebrews 13:5-6, *"'...I will never fail you, I will never abandon you.' So you can say with confidence, 'The Lord is my helper, so I will have no fear. What can mere people do to me?'"*

A thought to bloom by
Eve made a huge mistake when she ignored God's warning.

A verse to bloom by
And we know that God causes everything to work together for the good of those who love God and are called according to his purpose for them.

Romans 8:28

A prayer to bloom by

Abba, thank you for the privilege to call you Father and that I'm able to have an intimate relationship with you. You are the Father and Creator of all things and for that I am grateful. Abba, please forgive me if I have ignored your warnings in the past. I thank you ahead of time for the discernment to know when you are nudging me away from harmful decisions. In Jesus' name, amen.

APPLICATION QUESTIONS:

· When has God warned you about something, but you didn't listen?

· What happened?

CHAPTER THREE

KEEP ON BLOOMING

Even When Going Through Trials

Naomi stopped, turned and looked at her daughters-in-law. "No! This isn't right! You must go back to your families. You have no obligation to me now. You are still young and have the opportunity to marry again. Please, listen to me. I've been an old, selfish woman."

The three women traveling to Judah stopped in the middle of the road and clung to each other as they sobbed over the loss of their husbands. Orpah kissed Naomi and dried her mother-in-law's tear-stained cheek as she bade her good-bye to return to her loved ones in Moab.

"Ruth, you see Orpah has done what I asked of her. You, too, must return to your family," Naomi pleaded.

Ruth grabbed both of Naomi's gnarled hands and held them tightly in her own, as if their lives were now intertwined. "Please, Mother Naomi, don't ask me to leave you and turn back. Wherever you go, I'll go; wherever you live, I'll live. Your people will be my people, and your God will be my God. Wherever you die, I'll die, and there I'll be buried."

Naomi was overcome with gratitude. She hugged Ruth and held her at arm's length as she peered into the face of her angel, "Bless you child."

> But on the way, Naomi said to her two daughters-in-law, "Go back to your mother's homes. And may the Lord reward you for your kindness to your husbands and to me.
>
> *Ruth 1:8*

Our personalities and upbringings were so different. I had been thrust into adult situations early on and had developed an "I'm going to get it done or die trying" attitude, while Dallas had never been given the opportunity to accomplish any goals for himself.

Poor thing, he never had a chance to learn responsibility after we married, because I took over the reins of responsibility early on. I resented having to do it and he resented me doing it. Not a good combination to say the least.

The abuse started early in the marriage. There were times Dallas would say things in jest, but they weren't funny to me. They hurt. At the time, I couldn't give it a name, I just knew it didn't feel good. Now, I can call it by its ugly name: *emotional abuse.* I soon discovered he didn't like being around people or crowds. To say the least, this was disappointing to a young girl who loved people and had a new-found freedom to socialize. It wasn't what I expected married life would be.

I longed for someone to take care of me. Not another person to take care of. Despite being out of the house, my role as Mother's caregiver continued.

Mother's illness never abated. Hospital stays were still the norm. When I was seventeen and in my last year of high school, her doctor told her about a new procedure he thought she'd be a good candidate for – joint replacements.

Mother was ecstatic and went to Atlanta to have the procedures done. What they did to her was inhumane. In just six weeks' time they replaced both knees, both hips, and straightened her toes out by breaking them and putting metal bars through the end of her toes, hoping they would heal straight.

These procedures were still in the experimental stage and that's exactly what they did to her, experiment. After surgery, the pain was so great she had to take narcotics. Getting hooked on prescription pills is nothing new; this was in 1972. The very doctors who produced her pain refused to give her the pain relief she needed; making her go through methadone treatment instead.

After the surgeries, her health steadily declined. I felt guilty for leaving her alone to fend for herself as well as deal with Dad. Who would protect her? The larger question was – who would protect me? I knew, because of my religious upbringing, I was in it for the long haul. And I was, for the next twenty-six years.

I became pregnant with our first child, Erin, eleven months after we married. Erin was born in August of 1975. I felt as big as a whale by the time she decided to make her arrival. We fell in love with her the first time we laid eyes on her. I'd wanted a girl so much that when the nurse told me, I didn't believe her. But there she was, all whopping nine-and-a-half pounds of her. As someone once said, "Having a baby's like delivering a ham through your nose."

Unfortunately, neither of us were equipped to be good parents. We were up the creek without a paddle. How do we learn parenting? By imitating our parents. How did they learn parenting? By imitating their parents. You see how it can become a viscous cycle? Owner manuals come with every product we buy, but there are no owner manuals that come with our children.

The older I became the more I understood how much my parents loved me, and without a doubt, we loved our children. But because of strife that can invade a family, that love gets overshadowed. And for whatever reason, we tend to remember the negative things that happened in our lives over the positive.

When Erin was born we lived in a little apartment. Dallas worked third shift and slept during the day. Erin had colic for the first six months and cried incessantly. More than once, I sat and cried with her.

I begged Dallas to take a first-shift job, but he wouldn't. It was a bone of contention trying to keep Erin quiet while he slept. I don't think he appreciated it when I suggested he sleep at Mother's during the day until Erin outgrew the colic. That didn't happen.

When Erin was one, we moved closer to town into another little apartment. We weren't alone when we moved in. The roaches were so big you could have saddled and rode them. Let's just say it was an incentive to find a house.

When we moved into our house I had high hopes for a brighter future. Those hopes were soon dashed. Having children or getting a new house won't change someone. Dallas lost his job in law enforcement not long after we moved. The only time he ever bought me flowers was the day he came home and told me he didn't have a job. Turns out having words with your superior can have negative results.

Dallas was fired from several more jobs before finally landing a good job with the local power company. That's where he was working when our second daughter, Niki, was born. We fell in love all over again with this little sweetheart. She was born with a head-full of black hair long enough to comb into a Mohawk. Several months later, it fell out and grew back in white-blonde. We nicknamed her Cotton Top.

We attended church and I was involved as much as possible, but our home was not a happy home. I longed for a partner in parenting as well as someone to do fun things with. It didn't happen, and never happened while we were married.

Time flew by, and before I knew it Erin was entering second grade and Niki was starting preschool. Niki was a good baby from the beginning. Too good! She'd sleep all night and into the day if I let her. Fear gnawed at my insides. I knew this wasn't normal. I mentioned this to her doctor and he asked what I was complaining about. Niki didn't walk until she was almost one and a half, and when she did she stayed banged up from falling so much, including a broken thumb one time. We took her to a specialist in Atlanta, but were told there was nothing to worry about. Easy for them to say. Then when Niki was almost four, she began to have severe headaches, causing her to scream in pain until she threw up. After throwing up the pain went away. I knew something wasn't right – a mother's instinct.

Frantically, I called her doctor over the weekend and he rudely asked, "What do you want me to do? Start a case history over the phone?"

"No," I replied, "I want you to run tests to find out what's wrong."

Reluctantly, Niki's doctor admitted her to the hospital and scheduled her to have a CAT scan the next morning. When he made rounds the morning of the tests he said, "Ms. Malone, I don't treat behavior problems." Later that day, however, he would have to come back and tell me Niki had a malignant brain tumor. She was diagnosed with a Medulloblastoma, a childhood tumor. Those words changed our lives forever. My heart was yanked out of my body, and I cried out to God to spare my baby.

Naomi was a woman who knew the meaning of hardship and heartbreak. Many times Ruth's story has been told, and rightly so. Ruth was more like a daughter to Naomi than a daughter-in-law. But Naomi had her own story to tell.

> *In the days when the judges ruled in Israel, a severe famine came upon the land. So a man from Bethlehem in Judah left his home, taking his wife and two sons with him. The man's name was Elimelech, and his wife was Naomi. Their sons were Mahlon and Kilion.*
>
> *Ruth 1:1-2*

Ruth lived in Bethlehem of Judah, with Elimelech, her husband. Elimelech was the brother of a prince and lived a comfortable life for a time. But this was a dark time for Israel, "*...all the people did whatever seemed right in their own eyes*" (Judges 21:25).

The land was stricken with a famine, and Elimelech, deciding not to wait out the famine, took Naomi and their two sons and moved to the foreign land of Moab. The rest of Naomi's family remained behind in Israel.

I compare my own mother to Naomi, leaving everything behind to follow her husband to a small town in Georgia where he could find work. She, too, had two small boys at the time. All her family (and doctors) were left behind in Cincinnati where she had grown up. How hard that must have been for her, just as it was for Naomi.

> *Then Elimelech died, and Naomi was left with her two sons. The two sons married Moabite women. One married a woman named Orpah, and the other a woman named Ruth. But about ten years later, both Mahlon and Kilion died. This left Naomi alone, without her two sons or her husband.*
>
> *Ruth 1:3-5*

Not long after they arrived in Moab, Elimelech died. Naomi's heart was broken. Elimelech had insisted she leave her family behind and now she was alone in a foreign land. Did she become angry and cry out, "Why, why did you bring me to this God-forsaken land, and then die and leave me all alone?" as she pounded her fist into the dirt.

How many times I've cried out to God and asked similar questions, "Why, God, why Niki? Why did this have to happen to her, an innocent child?" I never heard an audible voice, but God's Word tells us over and over that this world is full of sorrow. *"How frail is humanity! How short is life! How full of trouble"* (Job 14:1).

I've concluded through study and prayer that there are just some answers we won't know until we reach heaven. God plainly tells us our ways are not his ways. But he's left us many words of comfort for those times when we feel like the very breath has been sucked from our being, and we can't go on. There have been many times when I've felt just like those dry bones in Ezekiel 37, convinced I'd die of heartbreak, and there was nothing anyone could have said to me at the time to make me think differently. Thank God, he has promised to bring us through those dark times.

In Romans 8:28, he left us with a beautiful promise. *"And we know that God causes everything to work together for the good of those who love God and are called according to his purpose for them."*

I admit, there have been times when I didn't understand how a situation could possibly work for good. But God made a promise, and I believe God keeps his promises. There are times when I needed to come out from the dark into the light before I could see where God had taken a devastating situation and caused something good to come from it.

Naomi, now a widow, was left with the responsibility to raise two sons. Since they were in the foreign land of Moab they had no choice but to marry Moabite women. Mahlon married Ruth and Kilion married Orpah. Things rocked along for about ten years until Mahlon and Kilion died. Once again, Naomi's heart was broken.

> *But Naomi replied, "Why should you go on with me? Can I still give birth to other sons who could grow up to be your husbands? No, my daughters, return to your parents' homes, for I am too old to marry again."*
>
> *Ruth 1:11-12*

After her sons' deaths, there wasn't anything keeping Naomi from returning to her homeland. She heard God had blessed Judah with good crops again. Naomi and her daughters-in-law set out on the journey. Somewhere along the way, Naomi decided to relinquish any hold she might have had on Ruth and Orpah from their feeling of duty to their mother-in-law. *"Go back to your mother's homes. And may the Lord reward you for your kindness to your husbands and to me"* (Ruth 1:8).

Ruth and Orpah were all she had left of her sons, and how comforting that must have been to Naomi, but maybe she began to feel guilty over her selfishness. Whatever the reason, she entreated them to return to their families. "You must go. I have nothing for you where I'm going. You need to find husbands from your own country," Naomi beseeched. It took all her strength not to relent and beg them to continue with her.

They broke down and wept. It was at this point Ruth refused to turn around and go back home. Orpah decided, through her tears, to return to her family. I don't know what I'd do in that situation, but I sure don't fault Orpah. I probably would have hugged Naomi, wiped my tears and turned right around and headed back home where everything I knew and loved existed.

But Ruth's reply has gone down in infamy, *"Don't ask me to leave you and turn back. Wherever you go, I will go; wherever you live, I will live. Your people will be my people, and your God will be my God. Wherever you die, I will die, and there I will be buried. May the Lord punish me severely if I allow anything but death to separate us!"* (Ruth 1:16-17).

Death! Are you serious Ruth? Yes, she was.

When they came to Bethlehem, the entire town was excited by their arrival. "Is it really Naomi?" the women asked. "Don't call me Naomi, she responded. "Instead, call me Mara, for the Almighty has made life very bitter for me."

Ruth 1:19-20

By the time Naomi and Ruth returned to Judah, Naomi was to the point of despair; what we would call depression today. And why shouldn't she be, she returned home destitute and without her husband or her two sons. The townspeople called out, "Is it really you Naomi?"

Naomi was so depressed she answered, "My name is not Naomi anymore. Just call me Mara. Life has served me a bitter blow. I left, having all I wanted or needed, now I return home empty handed and full of despair. Why has God sent such tragedy to me?"

Have you ever felt deep despair, or like life hasn't been fair to you? Most people will answer yes to this, and if they don't they probably will at some time in their life. But we don't have the monopoly on that kind of despair and depression. Many of our ancestors from the Bible have felt the same way at one time or another. There is not a human feeling Jesus didn't experience. Because of this he is able to intercede on our behalf with God.

One day Ruth the Moabite said to Naomi, "Let me go into the harvest fields to pick up the stalks of grain left behind by anyone who is kind enough to let me do it."

Ruth 2:2

With no way for the women to earn a living, Ruth went to a local field to glean the barley. This involved picking up leftovers after the harvesters cut down the stalks and tied them into bundles. Ruth was literally picking up scraps.

During my own journey, I've been to the point when the cupboards were bare. It was a frightening feeling. Ruth and Naomi must have felt that same desperation.

Ruth went out to gather grain behind the harvesters. And as it happened, she found herself working in a field that belonged to Boaz, the relative of her father-in-law Elimelech.

Ruth fell at his feet and thanked him warmly, "What have I done to deserve such kindness?" she asked. "I am only a foreigner."

"Yes, I know," Boaz replied. "But I also know about everything you have done for your mother-in-law since the death of your husband."

Ruth 2:3,10-11

While Ruth was working, Boaz came to check his fields. He noticed Ruth's beauty right away and asked his foreman, "Who is she?" The foreman told him how she'd come back to Judah with her mother-in-law, leaving behind her own family. Not only was he taken with her outer beauty, but he was impressed with her inner beauty as well. He let Ruth know how much he thought of her courageous sacrifice.

Ruth went home and excitedly told Naomi about Boaz. I can hear her now, "Oh, Naomi, I met the most handsome man today." She swooned a little as she spoke. "And not only is he good-looking, but he's a gentleman. His name is Boaz and he owns the fields." Ruth gazed into the distance, "Rich *and* handsome!" Then Ruth clamped her hand over her mouth. What had she done? Naomi was still grieving Mahlon, how unthoughtful of her. Ruth hoped this wouldn't push Naomi deeper into her depression?

> *One day Naomi said to Ruth, "My daughter, it's time that I found a permanent home for you, so that you will be provided for. Boaz is a close relative of ours, and he's been very kind by letting you gather grain with his young women. Tonight he will be winnowing barley at the threshing floor. Now do as I tell you – take a bath and put on perfume and dress in your nicest clothes. Then go to the threshing floor, but don't let Boaz see you until he has finished eating and drinking. Be sure to notice where he lies down; then go and uncover his feet and lie down there. He will tell you what to do."*
>
> *Ruth 3: 1-4*

But Naomi was as excited about the turn of events as Ruth. *"May the Lord bless him!"* Naomi told her daughter-in-law. *"He is showing his kindness to us as well as your dead husband. That man is one of our closest relatives, one of the family redeemers."*

"Ruth," Naomi suggests, "you've got to return to Boaz's fields, you'll be safe there and we need the food." Ruth continued working in Boaz's fields until the end of the harvesting season. Naomi hadn't been idle during that time – she had a plan up her robe.

"Ruth," Naomi said, "dress up in your prettiest dress – you know the blue one that makes your eyes sparkle. Then put on your best perfume and go to the threshing floor where Boaz will be working."

What in the name of all that was good was her mother-in-law thinking? Had she lost her mind? All this time Ruth had thought Naomi might be hurt by the attention she'd given Boaz. Now she wanted her to go and sleep at his feet? I don't know about you, but at this point I might have seriously questioned Naomi. But Ruth respected her mother-in-law and trusted her to do what was best for them. After all, Boaz was a relative of Naomi's. So, she put on her best dress and splashed on some perfume and set out to fulfill Naomi's plan.

> *So Boaz took Ruth into his home, and she became his wife.*
> *When he slept with her, the Lord enabled her to become*
> *pregnant, and she gave birth to a son.*
> *Ruth 4:13*

Naomi's plan worked and Ruth and Boaz were married. Ruth became pregnant and presented Naomi with a grandson they named Obed, who would become the father of Jesse and the grandfather of David.

> *Naomi took the baby and cuddled him to her breast. And*
> *she cared for him as if he were her own. The neighbor*
> *women said, "Now at last Naomi has a son again!" And*
> *they named him Obed. He became the father of Jesse and*
> *the grandfather of David.*
> *Ruth 4: 16-17*

Naomi was overcome with joy and happiness. Now she had a reason for living again. Time, and God, had turned around her circumstances. She couldn't see it when she returned to Judah brokenhearted. Remember, she even wanted to change her name to Mara. She probably thought she'd never be happy again. But even in her old age, she was renewed. Life wasn't over after all.

Don't ever give up hope. We can live through even the darkest times to enjoy happiness again.

A thought to bloom by

Naomi went through many devastating trials but never lost faith in God.

A verse to bloom by

Can anything ever separate us from Christ's love? Does it mean he no longer loves us if we have trouble or calamity, or are persecuted, or hungry, or destitute, or in danger, or threatened with death? No, despite all these things, overwhelming victory is ours through Christ, who loved us.

Romans 8:35, 37

A prayer to bloom by

Abba, I know that you have told us our days are few and full of sorrow. There are some days I have more trials than I think I'll be able to handle. But then I remember that you have not left me without a way to defeat the enemy. Through Jesus' death and resurrection, we have been given the victory. Thank you for the gift of your precious son. In Jesus' name, amen.

APPLICATION QUESTIONS:

- What is the time in your life when you've had the most trials?

- What were they?

- What helped you to get through them?

CHAPTER FOUR

KEEP ON BLOOMING

Even When You've Been Abused or Mistreated

Abigail hurriedly dismounted her donkey and fell at David's feet. "My Lord, please. Blame me." Abigail dared to look up at David. "I know Nabal is evil and mean as a snake, but please don't pay any attention to him. He's a fool, just as his name says."

Abigail used her wits to smooth things over with David. She apologized and begged his forgiveness if she had offended him in any way. Then she told him how smart he was by not letting the death of Nabal's household be a blemish on his record.

I'm sure Abigail wasn't the first, and won't be the last woman to attempt to mend what their foolish husbands have broken. Call Abigail a peacemaker. By calming David, she had just saved her whole household from his wrath, and certain death by his sword.

> *When Abigail saw David, she quickly got off her donkey and bowed low before him. She fell at his feet and said, "I accept all blame in this matter, my lord. Please listen to what I have to say. I know Nabal is a wicked and ill-tempered man; please don't pay any attention to him. He is a fool, just as his name suggests."*
>
> *1 Samuel 25:23-25*

One thing I'll never understand is why Niki's doctor didn't immediately send us to the much larger children's hospital in Atlanta, but instead, made arrangements for her to have the surgery in our small hometown where they really weren't equipped to handle this kind of procedure. Niki suffered because of that decision.

She spent the next week in the hospital while the neurosurgeon went on vacation. I remember one of the older nurses asking me if I was interested in having her transferred to the Atlanta hospital, but I didn't know it would mean better treatment for her. I wanted to stay near family and friends for support. I regret not pursuing it. That nurse obviously knew something I didn't.

Her surgery lasted all day. We waited anxiously for any news. The news wasn't good. The tumor was the size of a small orange and it was malignant. She would have to have further treatment.

We saw Niki while she was being wheeled into the intensive care unit. I've never seen anyone so pale. She had lost so much blood that they had to give her numerous transfusions. She talked a little and asked for a Sprite. That would be the last time I heard her talk for over three months.

After her initial surgery, Niki developed a bleed on the brain, and the neurosurgeon performed a second surgery to stop the bleeding.

When we went in to see her she was stiff and couldn't move. Within hours, we were told she had developed Meningitis from the surgery and her life was in grave danger. At death's door, they finally transferred her to Egleston Hospital in Atlanta, where one of the world's top pediatric neurosurgeons took over her care. By then, it was too late for Niki – her life would never be the same.

For the next three months, Niki remained in a coma as she fought for her life. She experienced high fevers, along with constant seizures, until they could find the right antibiotic to fight the infectious meningitis.

I was told by the doctor's assistant that it would be better if we put her in an institution. That she would never be better off than she was. Without hesitation, I told her Niki would be going home where she belonged. I didn't know, and didn't care, what long road lay ahead of us.

While she was in the coma she received very high doses of radiation for the cancer. Most children with a Medulloblastoma received chemotherapy, but the doctors knew she wouldn't survive the harsh treatment so they went with a high dose of radiation. Niki lost all her lovely cotton top from the radiation. My heart broke a little bit each time more hair fell into my hands with every brush-stroke. It never grew back to its original thickness.

There was a long narrow tunnel from the children's hospital to Emory Hospital where they gave the radiation treatments. Every day for over a month they would transfer Niki to a gurney and hook it to an electric cart that would pull her over. I rode in back of the cart as we wheeled down the hallways. It was daunting to me to hear the other carts fly by us. I can't imagine the panic Niki must have felt.

Up until this point, Niki had shown no signs of improvement. Once, when they transferred her to the table for her radiation, she bit the technician. Even though she couldn't see or speak, she was letting us know she was scared! We were ecstatic that she had the ability to bite. The technicians didn't feel the same way. They insisted she be tied down or sedated every day for treatment. We refused and said we'd take her somewhere else if they insisted she was treated this way.

During her stay, her neurosurgeon said she would need a shunt to drain the fluid off her brain that had collected due to the meningitis and surgeries. There was so much fluid the back of her neck had swollen into an alarming mass. The first shunt didn't work, so they had to do yet another surgery. After the second try the fluid subsided, and amazingly Niki's neck and head began to reshape. It was a beautiful sight.

She'd had so many surgeries her stomach went to sleep. She required a special medicine that cost thousands of dollars per treatment to keep her alive. It took several days before her stomach started working again.

I stayed with Niki round the clock except to go home, get clean clothes and visit with Erin. I felt guilty about leaving Erin, who was staying with her grandparents. It was reminiscent of me being alone when Mother went to the hospital.

I was twenty-seven at the time. I felt scared and alone most of the time while I was in Atlanta. Once, when I was with Niki for her radiation treatment, I decided to look at her chart that had been left on the gurney. I was reading it when a nurse yelled at me to put it down; I wasn't supposed to see it.

I was so startled and embarrassed, I dropped the chart. When I returned to her floor, I told one of Niki's nurses and she said I had the right to see it anytime I wanted to. They let me take it into Niki's room and read it. All the nurses that took care of Niki while she was in Atlanta were super. When the doctor in our hometown wrote his notes to the Atlanta doctor, he finished them up by writing in large letters, "Good luck, you're going to need it." It wasn't luck we needed, it was God.

After three months, Niki slowly, and I do mean slowly, woke up. Waking up from a coma isn't like in the movies where someone returns to their life like it never happened. Our four-year-old daughter had to learn everything again, including sucking. The nurses took a baby bottle nipple and taped it to a washcloth. Niki sucked on it until she was strong enough to drink from a straw. This took months.

The Niki who had been admitted to the hospital those many months before had died, and a new Niki was born. We loved her as much as ever, but we grieved for the Niki we lost. Niki's Aunt came to visit her one day. At this time, she hadn't been out of bed since her first surgery. I had to run an errand, and on the way back to Niki's room I saw a child sitting in a wheelchair who broke my heart. I thought, *how sad*. It was Niki. I went off by myself and cried when I realized my reaction to my own child.

After nearly four months in the hospital we brought Niki home. We had prepared her room with a hospital bed and all the equipment necessary to keep her alive. She still received liquid nourishment through a tube in her stomach. Even though she made great progress over the next year, sitting up and learning to eat, she would never be able to walk. Her balance had been destroyed.

While this was happening to our precious daughter, Mother's body was shutting down. When Niki was first admitted to the hospital, Mother had already been admitted and was one floor above Niki. The day after I was told Niki had a brain tumor, Dad came into our room and told me Mother had six weeks to live. She lived six months.

When we brought Niki home, she required twenty-four hour a day care. Our days were filled with doctor's visits and therapy sessions. During this time, I helped care for Mother. My days were full, but my heart was empty. I didn't understand why these things had happened to Niki. I never turned my back on God, but there were many times my faith waned and I longed for answers.

The changes in our life affected our entire family. So much time had to be devoted to Niki's care that Erin understandably felt slighted at times. None of us escaped unscathed.

A black cloud hung over us. Dallas withdrew further into himself and the abuse escalated. I became angry at the world. I longed for a healthy relationship with Dallas that would never happen.

Verbal abuse can be every bit as devastating as physical abuse. It tears you down from the inside out. It destroys your self-worth, makes you doubt your own ability to make decisions and leaves you a broken shell of yourself.

Many times I was told, "You're not good enough," or "Nobody will ever want you," and it wasn't unusual to hear, "I hate you."

I wanted to leave, but there were reasons I didn't. And it's the same for many women in this position. First, I was taught that you didn't get divorced unless infidelity was involved (which had been, but I didn't know at the time). Second, is the fear of the unknown. As bad as it was at home, at least I knew what I faced. I had no way of knowing what I would face on my own.

I also wondered who would help me take care of my girls. I was worn out most of the time just caring for Niki. How would I care for her and work to support us? I tried to leave several times, but fear and low self-esteem drove me back home. I thought surely he'd eventually leave, since he was the one who wanted out of the marriage – but he didn't.

Mother lived a few months after we brought Niki home from the hospital. It was heart wrenching to lose her, but I knew she didn't want to continue living in a body that was broken and worn out. After many years of suffering she would finally receive a body that was perfect. She received that glorified body when she turned fifty-four.

I attended Mother's funeral alone. At times like this, I was grateful for friends and family who supported me as much as they could.

Talk about an abusive husband – Nabal would not get the husband of the year award for sure! He's been described as boorish, churlish, uncouth, ill-mannered, and bad-tempered. And that's putting it nicely.

How true is the old edict "opposites attract?" I know it was true in my case. It would take another book to delve into the reasons why that happens, but for whatever reason, that was the case for Nabal and his wife Abigail.

She has been described as beautiful, politically astute, savvy, and wise. Abigail might be called the earliest pacifist on record.

Then David moved down to the wilderness of Maon. There was a wealthy man from Maon who owned property near the town of Carmel. He had 3,000 sheep and 1,000 goats, and it was sheep-shearing time. This man's name was Nabal, and his wife, Abigail, was a sensible and beautiful woman. But Nabal, a descendant of Caleb, was crude and mean in all his dealings.

1 Samuel 25:1-3

The story starts out with David being chased by his father-in-law, Saul, in the town of Maon, west of the Dead Sea. David, a wise man, wasn't riding alone. He brought along his secret service men for protection – all 600 of them. I kind of picture David and his entourage like Robin Hood and his Merry Men. As David traveled throughout the area, he made sure Nabal's men and sheep weren't harmed there in the wilderness where David and his men were camped.

It was sheep-shearing time at Nabal's farm; a time for celebration. Nabal, who loved his wine, was in high-cotton. He loved wine so much that it wasn't unusual for him to be drunk. David sent a messenger to ask Nabal if his men could join in the festivities, especially since he took care of Nabal's sheepherders.

"Who is this fellow David?" Nabal sneered to the young men. "Who does this son of Jesse think he is? There are

lots of servants these days who run away from their masters. Should I take my bread and my water and my meat that I've slaughtered for my shearing and give it to a band of outlaws who come from who knows where?"

1 Samuel 25:10-11

Nabal was very rich, but he wasn't too smart. He sent this reply to David. Let's just say, David was none too happy with that reply. In 1 Samuel 25:22 he vows his revenge, *"May God strike me and kill me if even one man of his household is still alive tomorrow morning!"*

Nabal had just signed his death warrant, and being the fool he was, didn't even realize it. One of Nabal's messengers went directly to Abigail and told her how he had responded to David's request.

Abigail wasted no time. She quickly gathered 200 loaves of bread, two wineskins full of wine, five sheep that had been slaughtered, nearly a bushel of roasted grain, 100 clusters of raisins, and 200 fig cakes. She packed them on donkeys and said to her servants, "Go on ahead. I will follow you shortly." But she didn't tell her husband Nabal what she was doing.

1 Samuel 25: 18-19

Behind the scenes Abigail went to work. She knew her husband had called trouble upon their household and she was out to correct his mistake. She gathered 200 loaves of bread, two wineskins full of wine, five sheep that had been slaughtered, nearly a bushel of roasted grain, 100 clusters of

59

raisins and 200 fig cakes. After all, she was feeding 600 men and one angry leader.

When she saw David, she fell at his feet and said, *"I accept all blame in this matter, my lord. Please listen to what I have to say"* (1 Samuel 25:24). I wonder why she thought she must take the blame. Was it because she had been abused and had taken the blame many times before when she had done nothing just to keep the peace?

> *David replies to Abigail, "Praise the Lord, the God of Israel, who has sent you to meet me today! Thank God for your good senses! Bless you for keeping me from murder and from carrying out vengeance with my own hands. For I swear by the Lord, the God of Israel, who has kept me from hurting you, that if you had not hurried out to meet me, not one of Nabal's men would still be alive tomorrow morning." Then David accepted her present and told her, "Return home in peace. I have heard what you said. We will not kill your husband."*
>
> *1 Samuel 25:32-35*

God used Abigail in a mighty way! David was in one foul mood. But thanks to Abigail's quick thinking, she saved many lives that day. How many times during their marriage had she interceded for Nabal's bad behavior? Did Abigail feel defeated when she returned home from saving her husband's life and found him drunk? Did she wonder, "Would it be this way forever?"

> *When Abigail arrived home, she found that Nabal was throwing a big party and was celebrating like a king. He*

*was very drunk so she didn't tell him anything about her
meeting with David until dawn the next day.*

1 Samuel 25:36

When she saw Nabal drunk she knew it wasn't a good time
to tell him she'd just fed his enemy. Having no desire to see
him worked into a rage, Abigail waited until morning, when
he was sober, and told him what she did. I can hear him bel-
lowing, "You did *what?*" I can just imagine how mad he was
when he found out Abigail had taken a bountiful meal to
David and his men. After all, hadn't he said "no?"

Abigail had proved herself to be stronger than Nabal had
given her credit for. I'm sure he thought she'd cowed down
and hidden when he went into his tirade and refused to invite
David and his men to the festivities.

*In the morning when Nabal was sober, his wife told him
what had happened. As a result, he had a stroke, and he
lay paralyzed on his bed like a stone. About ten days later,
the Lord struck him, and he died.*

1 Samuel 25:37-38

Abigail didn't have to live one more day with the tyrant
Nabal. When he heard what she'd done, he was struck with
an illness that paralyzed him. God struck him dead ten days
later. She had won her freedom. This would be a great ending
to the story, but there's more to come.

*When David heard that Nabal was dead, he said, "Praise
the Lord, who has avenged the insult I received from Nabal
and has kept me from doing it myself. Nabal has received*

61

*the punishment for his sin." Then David sent messengers
to Abigail to ask her to become his wife.*

1 Samuel 25:39

When David heard the news of Nabal's demise, he sent
messengers to Abigail to ask her to be his wife. She bowed low
to the ground and responded, *"I, your servant, would be happy to
marry David. I would even be willing to become a slave, washing the
feet of his servants!"*

I guess washing the feet of David's servants looked a whole
lot better than being married to Nabal.

And that, my friends, is what I call a happy ending!

A thought to bloom by

*Abigail was married to Nabal who was abusive, but she
persevered and God delivered her from her bondage.*

A verse to bloom by

*If you forgive those who sin against you, your heavenly
Father will forgive your sins.*

Matthew 6:15

A prayer to bloom by

*Abba, thank you for forgiving my sins and for the grace
that covers me. Thank you for your unconditional love. I
need your help, Abba. You've told us to forgive those who
have hurt us. I'm trying, I really am, but it's hard. I can't
do it without your help. Please show me how to forgive
like you've forgiven me so I can begin to heal. Help me to*

remember forgiveness is a gift to the one doing the forgiving. In Jesus' name, amen.

APPLICATION QUESTIONS:

- Have you ever been abused or mistreated?

- Have you forgiven this person so you could move on?

CHAPTER FIVE

KEEP ON BLOOMING

Even When You Don't Know What to Do

"Uncle Mordecai, please don't ask me to do this. The king hasn't summoned me, and if he doesn't hold out his scepter, I'll surely die."

Mordecai sent Esther this message. "Esther, if the King allows all Jews to be murdered, you'll die, too. Living in the palace won't save you. Who knows, maybe you were made queen to save your people."

Esther replied, "I'll do this, but gather all the Jews of Susa and pray and fast for me for three days. I'll do the same before approaching the king. If I must die, then I must die."

As a result of the king's decree, Esther, along with many other young women, was brought to the king's harem at the fortress of Susa and placed in Hegai's care.

Esther 2:8

Dallas continued to have problems at work, and I walked on eggshells. If I looked at him the wrong way, he exploded. Things flew through the air, and he kicked holes in doors or walls.

Eventually, he entered a hospital in Atlanta for treatment, where he stayed for three months. I was left to care for the girls and the household. I wasn't working, because most of my time was spent caring for Niki. With Dallas in the hospital, there wasn't much money coming in. There were times our pantry was empty and I had to ask people for help. It was one of the hardest things I'd ever done.

I was naive enough to believe when Dallas returned, he would be a brand new, improved version of himself and we would live happily ever after. It doesn't work that way with mental health issues – but I didn't know. Have you heard how many psychiatrists it takes to change a light bulb? It only takes one, but the light bulb's gotta *want* to change.

I read something once that was eye opening. Think about how hard it is to change something you want or desire to change about yourself. Why in the world do we ever think we can change somebody else?

I saw Erin dealing with her own depression, but I didn't have the emotional strength to give her the help and support she needed. How many times I wish I could go back and have a do-over as a parent.

Later, all I'd be able to do was tell her how sorry I was and to ask her forgiveness. I'm so thankful for the wonderful person she turned out to be, and that she's assured me many times over she's forgiven me.

I continued to cry out to God, "Where are you?" Amid the pain, I couldn't see him in those dark periods. Now in the light, I can look back and see the many times God provided for us, and the times he set angels in my path. Three of those angels are my friends, Beth and Vicki, and my sister-in-love, Anne. All the times I cried on their shoulders, not once did they turn their backs on me, and we're still good friends. Now that is a true friend – one who knows everything about you and still loves you.

I knew I'd have to go to work to help support us. I started slowly, working part time as a substitute teacher. I loved it! I worked in Special Education where Niki went to school – this kept me on the same schedule as the girls. Shortly thereafter, I started working full time as a paraprofessional in Special Education.

For years I'd been working with Niki physically and getting up several times during the night with her. Working in Special Education required lifting young adults; all of this eventually took a toll on my body and I developed aches and pains.

Someone suggested I see a chiropractor. I found one close to where we lived. I went in for an "adjustment," and by the next day I could barely walk, my lower back and legs hurt so bad. The next week I was scheduled for another visit. You'd think I'd have better sense than to go back to someone who had caused so much pain – nope, I marched right back in there and let him "adjust" my upper back. That was a mistake I would pay dearly for.

I woke up that night with spasms over my entire body. I was sure the elephant sitting on my chest would cause me to have a heart attack. I should have called the ambulance, but didn't. I toughed it out through the night. Think of the worse flu you've ever had and multiply your aches and pains ten times. It was a pain like I'd never experienced. I called to tell the chiropractor what had happened and I remember describing it as, "It feels like I have the flu." He asked if I wanted to come back in for another adjustment and by that time I'd learned my lesson and declined the invitation.

Let me say, I know this is not true of all chiropractors as many of my friends have been helped by their expertise. My situation was an unfortunate incident.

Vashti said, "Tell the king I will not be paraded around a group of drunken men."

> *In the third year of his reign, he gave a banquet for all his nobles and officials. He invited all the military officers of Persia and Media as well as the princes and nobles of the other provinces. The celebration lasted 180 days – a tremendous display of the opulent wealth of his empire and the pomp and splendor of his majesty.*
>
> *Esther 1:3-4*

King Xerxes the Great was the King of Persia during 486-465 B.C. He had thrown a feast for all the nobles and officials, as well as military officers, before going to war with Greece. The celebration lasted 180 days.

After the great feast, he held a banquet for all the people of the kingdom that lasted seven days. King Xerxes was in the courtyard surrounded by opulence. Drinks were served in gold goblets in various designs. By edict of the king, no limits were placed on the drinking. I imagine by the seventh day, the guests, as well as King Xerxes, were pretty much drunk.

> *King Xerxes told the seven eunuchs to bring Queen Vashti*
> *to him with the royal crown on her head. He wanted the*
> *nobles and all the other men to gaze on her beauty, for*
> *she was a very beautiful woman. But when they conveyed*
> *the king's order to Queen Vashti, she refused to come. This*
> *made the king furious, and he burned with anger.*
>
> *Esther 1:10-12*

It was in this drunken state King Xerxes called for Queen Vashti to be paraded before the nobles and other men to gaze on her beauty. In other words, he wanted to show her off. She wasn't having any part of it. She refused to come, which made the king furious. This was a time when women were seen and not heard, but for whatever reason she wanted no part in the king's plan to display her as he would display the jewels he wore in his beard, or the gold and silver couches in the garden. She stood her ground and would pay dearly for disobeying the king.

God's hand is evident throughout King Xerxes and Esther's story. The Jews lives were at stake and everything that happened during this time led to saving the Jewish nation and their lineage. The first occurrence we see is Queen Vashti refusing the king's request. This opened the door for Esther to become queen.

> *"What must be done to Queen Vashti?" the king*
> *demanded. "What penalty does the law provide for a*

queen who refuses to obey the king's orders, properly sent through his eunuchs?"

Esther 1:15

When Vashti refused the king's command, he was humiliated before his male guests. He gathered his advisers and asked, "The queen must be punished. What does the law say about a queen who refuses to obey the king's orders?" he demanded.

Well my goodness, King Xerxes pride was hurt. How dare the queen humiliate him before his friends. Obviously, he wasn't thinking how her pride would be hurt to be exhibited like a piece of property before a room full of ogling men.

But the queen's refusal caught the king off guard. She would have to pay for her insolence. Memucan, one of the king's advisers, put the wheels in motion for Vashti's punishment. During this period, women didn't disobey their husbands' requests. Now Vashti had the audacity to refuse the king – unheard of! Memucan pointed this out to the king, "Women everywhere will begin to despise their husbands when they learn that Queen Vashti has refused to appear before the king. It won't be long before all the wives throughout Persia will hear what the queen did and will start treating their husbands the same way." Merciful heavens, they were afraid of a women's uprising. All of this because Queen Vashti wanted to hold on to her dignity.

The advisers counseled the king to issue an edict that would banish Queen Vashti from the kingdom. Then, just in case another woman got any ideas about disobeying her husband, the king sent letters to all the provinces stating that every man should be ruler of his own house and should say whatever he pleases.

We've come a long way haven't we girls? Remember, this is not how God intended marriage to be. In Genesis, he tells us that male and female were made equal and that the two should become one. The people had strayed from God's desires.

> *So his personal attendants suggested, "Let us search the empire to find beautiful young virgins for the king. Let the king appoint agents in each province to bring these beautiful young women into the royal harem at the fortress of Susa...After that the young woman who most pleases the king will be made queen instead of Vashti."*
>
> *Esther 2:2-4*

Esther – enter stage left. The king appointed agents from each province to seek beautiful young virgins to bring them into his harem. The new queen would be chosen from those women. Mordecai, a Jew that worked at the palace in Susa, heard about the decree. He had a beautiful cousin, Esther, that he had adopted as a child when her parents died. Most likely, because of the age difference she called him *Uncle* Mordecai. On my father's side of the family I had cousins much older than me I called Aunt or Uncle out of respect, so this was plausible.

God had paved the way for Esther to save her people. Esther, along with many other women, was brought to the king's harem at Susa. Esther was placed in the care of the eunuch, Hegai. He was so impressed with her that she received special care from Hegai. He ordered her a special menu and provided her with beauty treatments. He, also, assigned her seven maids. Wow – sounds pretty good, right ladies? Unfortunately, this royal treatment came with a royal price.

Before each young woman was taken to the king's bed, she was given the prescribed twelve months of beauty treatments – six months with oil of myrrh, followed by six months with special perfumes and ointment.

Esther 2:12

Each girl received twelve months of beauty treatment – six months with oil of myrrh and six months with special perfumes and ointments. Well, they should be smelling pretty good by then. After the twelve months of treatment, each one was taken to the king's bed. Humph, those treatments don't sound so good now. Nonetheless, it came Esther's time to go into King Xerxes's private chambers. She obviously made a good impression on him. *"And the king loved Esther more than any of the other young women. He was so delighted with her that he set the royal crown on her head and declared her queen instead of Vashti"* (Esther 2:17).

During all this time, Esther kept her Jewish heritage under wraps. Mordecai had been keeping tabs on Esther and was pleased she'd been chosen for the new queen. One day while Mordecai was on duty at the king's gate, he overheard two of the king's eunuchs plotting to assassinate the king. He sent the information to Queen Esther who then told the king. Mordecai was given credit for saving the king's life and the two eunuchs were impaled on a sharpened pole. Not a good way to go.

Some time later King Xerxes promoted Haman son of Hammedatha the Agagite over all the other nobles, making him the most powerful official in the empire.

Esther 3:1

The plot thickens. King Xerxes had appointed Haman over all the nobles, making him the big wheel in the empire. And boy the power went straight to his head. He demanded that everyone he passed bow down to him. And everyone did, except Mordecai. He told Haman "I bow down to no one but my God."

This went on day after day while Haman's fury burned within him like hot coals in a fire. He wasn't about to let Mordecai off the hook, so to say. Haman approached the king and told him about a certain race of people who lived by their own set of laws and were separating themselves from everyone. These people refused to obey the laws of the king. Haman told the king, "It is not in the king's interest to let them live." Upon Haman's false testimony, King Xerxes agreed that they be destroyed.

> *When Mordecai learned about all that had been done, he tore his clothes, put on burlap and ashes, and he went into the city, crying with a loud and bitter wail.*
>
> Esther 4:1

On April 17th, the decree was sent out to the Provinces that all Jews, including women and children, would be killed on March 7th of the next year. A copy of the decree was issued and read to all the people. When Mordecai heard the horrific news, he tore his clothes, put on burlap and ashes, and went into the city, crying and wailing. Before long, all the Jews were mourning their fate.

> *Mordecai gave Hathach a copy of the decree issued in Susa that called for the death of all Jews. He asked Hathach to*

show it to Esther and explain the situation to her. He also asked Hathach to direct her to go to the king to beg for mercy and plead for her people. So Hathach returned to Esther with Mordecai's message.

Esther 4:8-9

Esther, unaware of the fate of her people, heard of Mordecai's condition and sent Hathach to find out why he was mourning. Along with a copy of the decree, he sent Hathach back to Esther, "Please go before the king and plead for mercy on our people."

This sounds like a reasonable request. After all, she was the queen. But it didn't work that way during Esther's time. Anyone who appeared in the king's inner court without an invitation was looking down the barrel of a gun. So Esther sent Mordecai another message, "You know anyone who appears before the king without an invitation will surely die unless the king holds out his gold scepter. And the king hasn't asked to see me in thirty days." If Esther appeared before the king there was a fifty-fifty chance she would die. Them odds don't look too good. From the tone of her message to Mordecai, Esther felt the same way.

Mordecai sent this reply to Esther: "Don't think for a moment that because you're in the palace you will escape when all other Jews are killed. If you keep quiet at a time like this, deliverance and relief for the Jews will arise from some other place, but you and your relatives will die. Who knows if perhaps you were made queen for just such a time as this?"

Esther 4:13-14

We've already learned Mordecai is strong-willed and he wasn't giving up. He replied to Esther, "Look, just because you live in the palace doesn't mean you'll escape. You'll die right along with your people." He didn't mince words! He needed to get the severity of the situation across to Esther. But it was likely his last words to her made the biggest impact. "Who knows if perhaps you were made queen for just such a time as this?" In other words, he was saying, "Perhaps God's hand has been in this all along."

> *Then Esther sent this reply to Mordecai: "Go and gather together all the Jews of Susa and fast for me. Do not eat or drink for three days, night or day. My maids and I will do the same. And then, though it is against the law, I will go in to see the king. If I must die, I must die."*
>
> Esther 4:15-16

Mordecai's words changed Esther's heart. After her fast, Esther donned her best robe and entered the inner court. Her life was literally on the line. She would either come out victorious or with a death sentence. Can't you just hear her sigh of relief when he held out the golden scepter toward her?

"What do you want Queen Esther? I'll give it to you, even if it's half my kingdom."

Esther was saving her real request for a more intimate time with the king. "I'd like to invite you and Haman to a banquet I've prepared in your honor."

The king wasn't fooled and knew she had something else on her mind. While they were at the banquet he asked her, "Now tell me what you really want."

So Haman's wife, Zeresh, and all his friends suggested,
"Set up a sharpened pole that stands seventy-five feet tall,
and in the morning ask the king to impale Mordecai on it.
When this is done, you can go on your merry way to the
banquet with the king."

Esther 5:14

Again, she asked the king and Haman to a banquet the next night. Haman was beyond ecstatic. The queen had requested his presence at a banquet for two nights in a row. There was only one thing that could bring down his spirits! You guessed it – Mordecai. On his way home, he passed Mordecai who again refused to bow down. Haman was so full of himself, that when Mordecai didn't bow he became furious. I'm surprised he didn't kill him right then and there. But he didn't, and proceeded to his home.

To soothe his bruised ego, he gathered his wife Zeresh and friends to boast about his position, his children, his wealth, and finally how the queen had invited him to the banquets. But then he complained, "And none of this means anything as long as Mordecai refuses to bow down to me."

Zeresh and his friends came up with a brilliant solution to his problem. "Set up a sharpened pole seventy-five feet high, and in the morning, ask the king for permission to impale Mordecai. Then you can go on your merry way." Haman was so pleased he ordered the pole set up. Little did he know God would have the last say.

That night the king had trouble sleeping, so he ordered an
attendant to bring the book of the history of his reign so
it could be read to him. In those records he discovered an

*account of how Mordecai had exposed the plot of Bigthana
and Teresh, the two eunuchs who guarded the door to the
king's private quarters. They had plotted to assassinate
King Xerxes.*

Esther 6:1-2

In place of warm milk, King Xerxes called for an attendant
to read from the history book of his reign. It was no coinci-
dence the attendant read the account of Mordecai's bravery.
King Xerxes asked, "What reward did we give Mordecai for
saving my life?"

"Nothing yet, sir."

Haman had just arrived at the outer court to ask the king
for permission to impale Mordecai, when the king asked who
was in the outer court.

*So the attendants replied to the king, "Haman is out in
the court."*

*"Bring him in," the king ordered. So Haman came in,
and the king said, "What should I do to honor a man who
truly pleases me?"*

Esther 6:5-6

When he discovered it was Haman the king invited him
in and asked his advice on the reward for someone who truly
pleases the king. Haman couldn't see beyond his nose and
assumed the king meant him. So he laid it on thick: "He should
bring out one of the king's royal robes and a royal horse he has
ridden on. Take the one who pleases the king and lead him
through the city square having the official shout as they go,
'This is what the king does for someone he wishes to honor!'"

"Excellent idea! Quick, get my robe and horse and do this for Mordecai. And don't leave out a thing you've suggested!"

I can only imagine the look on Haman's face - priceless. But he had no choice than to do what the king suggested for Mordecai. He was complaining to Zeresh and his friends when the king's eunuchs came and whisked him away to the queen's banquet.

> *So the king and Haman went to Queen Esther's banquet. On this second occasion, while they were drinking wine, the king again said to Esther, "Tell me what you want, Queen Esther. What is your request? I will give it to you, even if it is half the kingdom!"*
>
> *Esther 7:1-2*

While they were at the banquet relaxing and sipping wine, the king asked Esther what she really wanted. She revealed to him that she was a Jew and her people were in danger. "For my people have been sold to those that would kill, slaughter and annihilate us."

"Who'd do such a thing?" the king asked.

"Wicked Haman, who is our adversary and our enemy."

King Xerxes was so angry he walked off into his garden. While he was gone, Haman fell on the couch where Queen Esther was reclining and pleaded for his life. He was there when the king returned. "Will you assault the queen right in front of me?" The King immediately ordered Haman's death. When the king found out about the pole Haman had erected for Mordecai, he demanded Haman be impaled on the very pole he had built for Mordecai.

On that same day King Xerxes gave the property of Haman, the enemy of the Jews, to Queen Esther. Then Mordecai was brought before the king, for Esther had told the king how they were related. The king took off his signet ring – which he had taken back from Haman – and gave it to Mordecai. And Esther appointed Mordecai to be in charge of Haman's property.

Esther 8:1-2

The king replaced Haman with Mordecai and asked about the decree ordering the death of the Jews. The king's hands were tied because once the king's seal had been placed on a decree, it couldn't be rescinded. However, one could be written to counteract the old one. King Xerxes ordered Mordecai to write the decree however he wanted. The decree was written so that all Jews would be able to defend themselves if they were attacked.

When the time came for the execution of the Jews, they thwarted the attack. Esther had saved the Jewish nation!

Even though it's easy to see God working throughout this story, it's evident Esther couldn't feel his intervention while she was in a fight for her life, "If I must die, I must die." How many times have we been in dark places and felt alone, but when we came out into the light and looked back, recognized how God had been there all along?

A thought to bloom by

God had a plan to use Esther. It took her a while, but eventually she discovered what it was and how she could cooperate with him.

A verse to bloom by

"For I know the plans I have for you," says the Lord.
"They are plans for good and not for disaster, to give you
a future and a hope."

Jeremiah 29:11

A prayer to bloom by

Abba, sometimes I'm confused about what I'm supposed
to do. I know you're always working in my life, but there
are times I don't see it until the crisis has past. Thankfully
you remind us in Jerimiah you have plans for us and those
plans are for our good – not to harm us. Help me to see
your hand in my life during the hard times as well as the
good times. In Jesus' name, amen.

APPLICATION QUESTIONS:

· Have you ever gone through a time when you didn't
know what God wanted you to do?

· How did you discover what to do?

CHAPTER SIX

KEEP ON BLOOMING

Even When You're Desperate

"Please don't make me go, Mother. I don't know Er, and you've heard all the stories about him. He's a mean and evil person. Please!"

"Daughter, you don't have a choice. Your father's already agreed to let you marry Er, and Judah is here to take you back to their camp. There is no room for negotiation. And crying will get you nowhere with your father." She grabbed Tamar with both hands and spun her around to face her, "Do you understand. Peace between these two families is on your shoulders now."

> *In the course of time, Judah arranged for his firstborn son,*
> *Er, to marry a young woman named Tamar. But Er was*
> *a wicked man in the Lord's sight, so the Lord took his life.*
> *Genesis 38:6-7*

My aches and pains never went away. After many tests, I was finally diagnosed with Fibromyalgia, triggered from the trauma caused by the chiropractor. I've often wondered if I had been predisposed because of Mother's arthritis. The greatest fear my pain caused was not being able to care for Niki, because her care required so much physical ability. Within weeks, I knew I'd no longer be able to work in Special Education because I couldn't continue with the required lifting. I could barely care for Niki.

I wasn't given much sympathy on the home front. One time when I was in the bathroom, sick and throwing up, Dallas came and banged on the door, demanding I get out so he could use it. This wasn't unusual behavior for him. It became the norm.

I'd been going to counseling for years, but it's hard to work on a marriage by yourself. I begged him to go with me, so we piled in the car with the kids and headed to the counselor's office. Again, I had high hopes.

All of us sat in her office as she looked at Dallas and asked, "Well, how do you feel about being here?"

He looked directly into her eyes and said, "I didn't want to come and I don't want to be here." With that he got up and walked out, leaving the counselor and me dumbfounded. I don't know why it surprised me. As tears streamed down my cheeks, I quietly told her I supposed there wasn't any use in having a session that day. She agreed. She finally saw what I'd been trying to tell her.

Dallas went through a period when he would hang out the window and shoot squirrels in the back yard. We lived in a subdivision. The houses were very close to each other, so when the squirrels didn't die right away, they'd go next door and die. I was out back one day when my neighbor leaned over the fence and asked me if I knew what was happening to the squirrels. I was so embarrassed I wanted to die right then and there. I told her, "No, I don't know." Of course, it was a lie.

I was so happy when I met her later in life and could tell her what had really happened to the squirrels. I had a feeling she already knew.

Once Dallas called me to come look at something out the kitchen window. I thought it might be some birds at the bird feeder. Instead, I saw a dead squirrel hung by the neck from a tree limb. When he saw my expression, he cackled the evilest laugh and said, "I guess I'd better get it down before the neighbors get home from work." Bile rose in my throat, and fear gripped me with clawed hands. It was as if he was saying, "This is what could happen to you."

In 1995, three years after being diagnosed with Fibromyalgia, I decided to go back to school and earn an associate's degree in Human Services. It was also during this time I decided to resume counseling. This was a turning point in my life. I began to see things through different eyes. Even though I was in a lot of physical and emotional pain, I realized I could continue to grow and accomplish goals. Even while facing challenges. Thus, I was determined to bloom in my broken places!

I also searched deep within and began to depend on God to meet my needs. I credit much of this change to Vicki, who also has a daughter with special needs. She showed me by example that you can still live your life, laugh, and have fun despite the challenges of being a caregiver. And that's what we did with the girls. But, mostly she taught me about having faith in God.

Through prayer, talking with Vicki, watching her deep faith, and reading encouraging materials she gave me, I came to learn about a different God than I had grown up with. She introduced me to a loving, caring and grace-filled God.

This didn't happen overnight. I spent years letting go of the beliefs I'd been taught. It was scary, because our beliefs make up who we are. If we let go of them and start over, then we're letting go of who we thought we were for many years. But the results can be miraculous. I began to read and learn about a God that loved me and wanted the best for me. Even if I didn't always understand why I had to bear the trials of life. God never promised life would be easy, but he did promise he'd always be with me. In Hebrews 13:5 God said, *"Never will I leave you; never will I forsake you."*

While I was in school, I took a creative writing course. Besides my early love of reading, this sparked a fire in me to write. While fulfilling an internship at an agency that helped families in need of guidance, one of my co-workers offered to sell me a computer, monitor, and keyboard for fifty dollars.

Now, mind you, I didn't question why she was selling the computer for such a low price – until I got it. Let's just say I christened it "Dino" – you know, for dinosaur. I didn't care that it worked on the old DOS operating system, and that the computer and monitor took up the whole desk. I was elated when I discovered Office Depot still had dot-matrix printers. None of this mattered to a budding writer. I wrote many poems and short stories on ole Dino.

I entered one of my first short stories into the yearly Guidepost writing contest. I didn't win, but I received a letter from one of the editors advising me my manuscript had been considered. This was enough encouragement to keep me writing.

Family life continued to go downhill at home. Erin was nearly twenty and had moved to Atlanta to work and go to school. Finally, after many years of changing jobs or missing work, Dallas quit the power company – this would be the last time he worked. During the next year, while waiting on disability to go through for his mental health issues, we had no income. His parents helped us until we could pay them back. I look back and realize how God always provided what we needed – not what we wanted, by far, but we always had the basics. We never went hungry, or without necessities.

With Dallas staying at home all the time, the abuse became unbearable. I was in my fourth year of college by this time. I worked part time, went to school, and took care of Niki.

I kept journals in some of my darkest times. When I began writing about my journey, I dug through old boxes to find them. I thought there was only one journal, but I discovered I'd filled two notebooks covering three years. As I read the posts, my heart ached for this Debbie. It was evident by the following post that she didn't know how to take care of herself.

I think I have finally found someone who is willing to take care of me. They said I needed to be patient with them though, because this was new to them and they didn't know what all my needs were yet. They might be awkward at first, and maybe make some mistakes, but if I would trust them and give them a chance they wanted to be my partner for life. They felt sure working together I would have a happier, healthier life. Her name – Debbie.

When you're in an abusive relationship you lose so much: confidence, self-esteem, decision-making abilities, self-worth, as well as the ability to care for yourself.

One theme that ran throughout the journals was the hope that I would continue to grow stronger emotionally and in my walk with God. I never gave up on a better life.

It was during this period I left several times with the intentions of never going back, but would end up back home. The guilt I had of returning to a horrible situation was devastating. I remember my therapist telling me there would be a day when nothing would make me go back. She was right – that day would eventually arrive.

We know from history that Judah was a man to be reckoned with. Yes, he saved his brother Joseph's life, but he was in on the scheme to get rid of Joseph, and then told their father he was killed by a wild animal. He had a shady past.

In the course of time, Judah arranged for his firstborn son, Er to marry a young woman named Tamar.

Genesis 38:6

Judah arranged for his oldest son Er to marry a Canaanite woman named Tamar. Even though this was common practice, Tamar's fear of the unknown must have been overwhelming.

It was known throughout the land that Er was a wicked man. I can hear the pleas of this young lady begging her mother, "Please, Mother, don't make me go." Her pleas fell on deaf ears and she left with Judah to return and marry Er. But Er was so wicked that God took his life.

> *But Er was a wicked man in the Lord's sight, so the Lord took his life.*
>
> Genesis 38:7

He must have been pretty atrocious for God to snuff out his life. Was he abusive to Tamar? My guess is he was. Someone so wicked that God took his life wouldn't think twice about hurting a woman. Tamar had lost much in a short time. She'd lost her identity, her home, and now she'd lost her husband. She has no one to support her.

> *Then Judah said to Er's brother Onan, "Go and marry Tamar, as our law requires of the brother of a man who has died. You must produce an heir for your brother.*
>
> Genesis 38:8

Once again, Tamar had no choice in the matter. The law at the time was known as the Levirate Law. A Levirate marriage is a type of marriage where the brother of a deceased man is obliged to marry his brother's widow, and she is obliged to be married to her deceased husband's brother. This was done to keep the bloodline in the family alive. The child from this union would receive the deceased brother's inheritance. I don't think Onan, Er's next brother in line to be married, liked this plan too much.

But Onan was not willing to have a child who would not be his own heir. So whenever he had intercourse with his brother's wife, he spilled the semen on the ground.

Genesis 38:9

"No way!" Onan said. "I want my own heir." So he decided he'd make sure Tamar didn't get pregnant with his child. It seems God wasn't too happy with that decision, either.

But the Lord considered it evil for Onan to deny a child to his dead brother. So the Lord took Onan's life, too.

Then Judah said to Tamar, his daughter-in-law, "Go back to your parents' home and remain a widow until my son Shelah is old enough to marry you." (But Judah didn't really intend to do this because he was afraid Shelah would also die, like his two brothers.) So Tamar went back to live in her father's home.

Genesis 38:10-11

How humiliating for Tamar. Still a young woman, she had already lost two husbands and had no children. When she returned home instead of receiving a welcome from the family, her father yelled at her, "Tamar! You have brought shame to this household. I sent you to bear sons and bridge peace between these two families, and now Judah doesn't even want you in his household."

But the abuse doesn't stop there. Tamar's mother is no less harsh with her words, "What will you do now Tamar. You have no husband and no prospect of one in the future. You must remain chaste until Judah sends for you. Now that he has lost two sons that were married to you, do you think he wants to lose a third? You will be a burden to your father," Tamar's mother shook her head. "You can't seem to do anything right!"

Tamar found herself in quite the predicament. She's lost two husbands and everyone thought she had something to do with their deaths. Judah promised her when Shelah became old enough to marry that he would send for her. The Bible tells us he had no intention of doing so. But Tamar's hope never waned.

> *Tamar was aware that Shelah had grown up, but no arrangements had been made for her to come and marry him.*
>
> Genesis 38:14

We aren't told what happened, but the light bulb in Tamar's mind finally lit up. Maybe she saw Shelah in the marketplace with his friends. He was a grown man with a beard – plenty old enough to marry and father children. Her heart broke again.

According to the Levirate law, if the brother of the widow's dead husband is too young, the father can step in and take the place of the brother, but if he chooses not to do so, the widow could be free to marry again. All this time, Tamar had remained faithful to Judah's family by waiting for Shelah. Judah could have released her, but he kept her captive with his promise.

The tears were so many it was hard for Tamar to see her way home. Her sadness simmered and grew into anger. *How dare Judah deprive me of my right to have children?* Tamar knew her parents would be of no help to her in this matter. She had to find a way for Judah to fulfill his promise.

So she changed out of her widow's clothing and covered herself with a veil to disguise herself. Then she sat beside the road at the entrance to the village of Enaim, which is on the road to Timnah. Judah noticed her and thought she was a prostitute since she had covered her face.

Genesis 38:14-15

Tamar had learned Judah's wife had died. After his time of mourning, Judah and his friend Hirah traveled to Timnah to supervise the shearing of his sheep. Someone told Tamar, "Look, your father-in-law is going up to Timnah to shear his sheep." Her plan was devised. Tamar was at the point of desperation. We've all been there ladies, at one time or another, right? Tamar knew for sure that Judah had no intention of letting Shelah marry her, which meant she would be a chaste widow the rest of her life. And being alone would also leave her vulnerable. When a woman reached old age, it was expected that her children would take care of her, but Tamar would be alone. Out of this desperation came her plan to dress up like a temple harlot and trick Judah as he journeyed to Temnah.

Judah noticed her and thought she was a prostitute, since she had covered her face. So he stopped her and propositioned her. "Let me have sex with you," he said, not realizing that she was his own daughter-in-law. "I'll send you a young goat from my flock," Judah promised.

"But what will you give me to guarantee that you will send the goat?" she asked.

"What kind of guarantee do you want?" he asked.

She answered, "Leave me your identification seal and its cord and the walking stick you are carrying." So

Judah gave them to her. Then he had intercourse with her, and she became pregnant. Afterward she went back home, took off her veil, and put on her widow's clothing as usual.

Genesis 38:15-19

It had been years since Judah had seen Tamar, plus she was wearing a veil. He didn't recognize her. Because of his lust he became the fly in Tamar's web. The Bible doesn't tell us much about Tamar's personality, but we're left with the impression this scheme is out of character for her. If she'd been given her rightful place as Shelah's wife, or if Judah had freed her, she would not have turned to such drastic measures. She made the decision to have Judah's children for her survival. We can debate the question, if her decision was right or wrong, but how many times have we made decisions out of desperation?

About three months later Judah was told, "Tamar, your daughter-in-law, has acted like a prostitute. And now, because of this, she is pregnant."

"Bring her out and let her be burned!" Judah demanded.

But as they were taking her out to kill her, she sent this message to her father-in-law. "The man who owns these things made me pregnant. Look closely. Whose seal and cord and walking stick are these?"

Judah recognized them immediately and said, "She is more righteous than I am, because I didn't arrange for her to marry my son Shelah."

Genesis 38:24-26

Tamar must have felt like an old-timey washing machine – churning with a plethora of emotions when she found out she was pregnant. One minute she asked herself, "What have I done?" The next minute she is elated to be pregnant with Judah's child. She would have the child she had been deprived of from Judah's lineage. But her worst fear was what would happen to her when she couldn't hide it anymore and others found out. If a woman was found in adultery, death was imminent. Yep, it was the old double standard. It was normal for men to have more than one wife, while women were expected to remain faithful to their husband. Having Judah's child was not a spur of the moment decision. She had wittingly planned to get items from Judah that would identify him for just this reason.

When Judah was told Tamar was pregnant, in all his righteous indignation he demanded Tamar be burned to death. We already know Judah wasn't free from his own sins that haunted him, but he was quick enough to condemn Tamar. It brings to mind the verse in Matthew 7:3, *"And why worry about a speck in your friend's eye, when you have a log in your own."*

Tamar felt the flames from the roaring fire. Everyone stood around just waiting for this harlot to be burned at the stake. But Tamar had one more trick up her sleeve. She asked a messenger to hurry and send the items she had acquired to her father-in-law. "Tell him whoever owns these things is the father of my child. Run as fast as you can, my life depends on it."

I would have loved to have seen the expression on Judah's face – one of complete shock. The prostitute he'd been with was really his daughter-in-law. Essentially the items she sent to Judah said, "Gotcha!"

His heart was pricked. He knew without a doubt he had wronged Tamar by denying her place into his family. Without hesitation he said these words, "She is more righteous than I, because I didn't arrange for her to marry my son Shelah."

When Tamar's time came she delivered not one son, but two. She named them Perez and Zerah. Tamar's decision allowed her to protect the lineage, giving birth to twins, Perez and Zerah. She thus restored two sons to Judah, who had lost Er and Onan to their sins against God. Perez became a direct ancestor of King David, and later, Jesus Christ.

Tamar's solution to her problem may not have been what you or I would have done, but her decision was born from the necessity to survive. It was the best one she knew to make. And one of her sons, Perez, is in the lineage of Jesus. God can take decisions we've made from desperation, which might not have been the greatest of decisions, and turn them around for good.

Come on girls, we've all walked in Tamar's shoes at one time or another where we didn't make the best decision. But that's all right, because our God can take that tattered mess and turn it into a beautiful quilt that represents our life!

A thought to bloom by
Tamar lost everything and made a bad decision out of her desperation.

A verse to bloom by
The Lord says, "I will guide you along the best pathway for your life. I will advise you and watch over you."

Psalm 32:8

A prayer to bloom by

Oh, Abba, there are so many times I've made bad decisions out of desperation. I need your hand to guide me and watch over me. Help me depend on you and go to your Word for guidance when I feel desperate or panicked. Thank you for giving us a road map to life – your Word. In Jesus' name, amen.

APPLICATION QUESTIONS:

- When have you made a decision out of desperation?

- What was it?

- What happened as a result?

CHAPTER SEVEN

KEEP ON BLOOMING

Even When Your Life is a Mess

"Yes, they were here earlier. I had no idea where they were from. At dusk, right before the gates closed, they left the city." Rahab looked towards the direction of the gates, "If you hurry, you can probably catch up with them."

The day Dallas threw a cup at me so hard it cut a hole in the wall and stuck there would be my last day in the same house with him. The cup came so close to my head I heard it whiz by. When Dallas said he was about to knock me into the middle of next week – I believed him. After twenty-six years of marriage, I knew if I didn't leave, I wouldn't leave alive.

It was now or never. I left with my computer, a few clothes, and my schoolbooks. I was in my last semester of college toward earning my Bachelor's degree. I was emotionally and physically sick when I moved in with Dad. He lived in a small mobile home (think tiny house) and by now was in his eighties. I didn't have the ability at the time to take care of Niki by myself, so I still relied on her dad to help. She spent some of the time with Dallas and some with me.

In May of 1999, within a few days of each other, I graduated from college, turned 45, and my divorce became final.

Going through the divorce was a curve in the road that almost made me wreck. I refused to file for divorce when Dallas was the one who wanted out of the marriage, so I left that up to him. Being divorced was the lowest time in my life, next to when Niki had gotten sick.

I wanted Niki to live with me, so after I graduated I moved into low-income housing so we'd have more room.

The little apartment was newly renovated and I fixed it up as homey as possible. But it wasn't home! The neighbors in my complex were nice to us, but they had their own problems to deal with. I'll never forget being woken up from a dead sleep hearing screams from the woman upstairs. I knew for sure she was being murdered. It wasn't quite that bad; her boyfriend had told her he was leaving and she responded by screaming. But it was enough to rattle my nerves. I knew this wasn't a healthy place for us.

The straw that broke the camel's back came when I was on the phone with my brother. He had his police scanner on and heard a call for backup at the complex next to mine. Somebody was holed up in one of the apartments with a gun threatening to shoot if they tried to restrain him. I told my brother while we were talking, "I will not live here any longer." I went the next day and asked Dad if we could move back in with him. I thought this was the lesser of two evils. He agreed, and Niki and I moved into his little mobile home. She slept on the bed and I slept on the couch – but I didn't care. At least we were out of immediate danger.

After a few months, Dad and I pooled our resources and traded the tiny mobile home for a double wide. We had bought ourselves a mansion! Niki and I had our own bedrooms and a bath to share between us. I hadn't gotten much money from the divorce, you can't get blood from a turnip, but what little I had served to provide Niki, Dad and I a suitable home.

Dad was not in good health. I slid right back into the role of caregiver. Dad was a veteran and to get his veteran's health care we had to travel to Atlanta to the VA Hospital. I dreaded those trips. The hospital was huge and we walked from one end to the other to get to his doctor's appointments. I usually pushed him in a wheelchair because he couldn't walk the entire time.

Which reminds me of the time his little dog Pepe chewed his hearing aid for the umpteenth time. I just went into my room, closed the door and cried. Dad said, "Don't worry Debbie, we can go to the VA and get another one." It's funny now, but it sure wasn't then.

It had been a long time since I'd lived at home and dealt with Dad's strong-willed nature. When I moved in with him again, it became apparent he hadn't changed much. Things had to be done his way – or the highway. Even though it was somewhat different from being with Dallas, I felt I was in another abusive situation. At least I knew Dad cared about me, but I pretty much lived in my room when I was at home. Niki and I just stayed on our end of the house.

Here's an example of Dad's stubbornness. He had broken his hip and the doctor told him not to put any pressure on that leg for three months, and not to drive until he was released. The morning after he returned home from surgery, I heard the car start up at six a.m. I jumped up, looked out the window and saw Dad's car going down the driveway and tail lights fading in the early morning fog.

Then Joshua secretly sent out two spies from the Israelite camp at Acacia Grove. He instructed them, "Scout out the land on the other side of the Jordon River, especially around Jericho." So the two men set out and came to the house of a prostitute named Rahab and stayed there that night.

Joshua 2:1

After Moses' death, Joshua took over as leader of the Israelite people. They had yet to enter the Promised Land, so Joshua sent out two spies on a reconnaissance mission to check out Jericho. This was the last big obstacle between the Hebrews and the Promised Land. There they met an unlikely ally – Rahab.

There has been an on-going debate among scholars as to whether Rahab was really a prostitute or perhaps an inn-keeper who could be at times less than scrupulous. However, the word zanah in Hebrew translates into prostitute.

But as we've discovered throughout this study, God chose to use people who were broken or had flaws – like so many humans. Personally – I don't know anyone who is perfect. And God used Rahab in a mighty way to help the spies Joshua had sent to retrieve information they would need to fight and overtake the people of Jericho.

As you continue to study Rahab you'll see she was already familiar with God and had great reverence for him. She wanted to help God's cause, but she also had an ulterior motive. She wanted to save her family from destruction.

> *But someone told the king of Jericho, "Some Israelites have come here tonight to spy out the land." So the king of Jericho sent orders to Rahab, "Bring out the men who have come into your house for they have come here to spy out the whole land."*
>
> Joshua 2:2-3

It was night. Someone was banging on the door and Rahab's heartbeat revved into double-time. *Are the men safely hidden?* She opened the door to find three soldiers holding torches. They moved in closer to get a better look at her face. She smelled the vile breath of the soldiers.

"Where are they?" the big one growled.

Another man shoved his torch closer and looked Rahab in the eyes, "Yeah, we know they're here. We've been told they were seen entering your house. If you know what's good for you, you'll tell us where they are!"

Rahab's heart beat so fast she feared they could hear each thump. She had to be strong – her life and her family's depended on the men she had welcomed into her home. She hoped they were well hidden. *Think quick, Rahab!*

She gathered unseen strength and spoke with a bravado she didn't possess. "You're right. They were here earlier, but I didn't know where they were from. They left around dusk, before the city gates closed." Rahab looked toward the gate like they might still be there. "You might be able to catch them if you hurry."

Rahab knew this God she had heard about was with her that night, because the three soldiers turned around and left.

Actually, she had taken them up to the roof and hidden them beneath bundles of flax she had laid out. So the king's men went looking for the spies along the road leading to the shallow crossings of the Jordan River. And as soon as the king's men had left, the gate of Jericho was shut.

Before the spies went to sleep that night, Rahab went up on the roof to talk with them. "I know the Lord has given you this land," she told them. "We are all afraid of you. Everyone in the land is living in terror. For we have heard how the Lord made a dry path for you through the Red sea when you left Egypt.

Joshua 2:6-10

"Now swear to me by the Lord that you will be kind to me and my family since I have helped you. Give me some guarantee that when Jericho is conquered, you will let me live, along with my father and mother, my brothers and sisters, and all their families."

Joshua 2:12-13

This was a win-win situation for Rahab. Because she had helped the spies, she knew they would probably help her in return.

"Look, I've helped you in your time of need. It would have been easy for me to just tell them where you were, but I risked my life to save yours. I know you'll use the information you gather from your mission to destroy all the people of Jericho. I'm asking not only for me, but the lives of my family to be spared. You owe me that much in return." Rahab didn't mince words. She'd just risked her life so they could take their intelligence report back to Joshua. They now knew the city was terrified of them.

Rahab held her breath while she waited for their answer to her bold request.

> We offer our lives as a guarantee for your safety," the men agreed. "If you don't betray us, we will keep our promise and be kind to you when the Lord gives us the land."
>
> Then since Rahab's house was built into the town wall, she let them down by a rope through the window.
>
> Before they left, the men told her, "We will be bound by the oath we have taken only if you follow these instructions. When we come into the land you must leave this scarlet rope hanging from the window through which you let us down. And all your family members – your father, mother, brothers, sisters and all of your relatives – must be here inside the house... If you betray us, however, we are not bound by this oath in any way."
>
> "I accept your terms," she replied. And she sent them on their way, leaving the scarlet rope hanging from the window.
>
> Joshua 2:14-21

They agreed to Rahab's terms; her family would be safe. But there was a stipulation. She must let them know which one was her house by hanging a red rope from her window and her family must all stay within the house. A small price to ask for her family's lives.

> *Then the two spies came down from the hill country, crossed the Jordan River, and reported to Joshua all that had happened to them. "The Lord has given us the whole land," they said, "for all the people in the land are terrified of us."*
>
> *Joshua 2:23-24*

It wasn't just Rahab that had been terrified of the soldiers. The spies were probably shaking in their sandals while Rahab talked to the three soldiers. Would she give them up? Would they swarm the house and find them hidden in the flax? They couldn't wait to leave and share the good news with Joshua.

According to the Word, Rahab was in a hot mess. She was a prostitute. Would God dare use such a woman in his plan to lead the Israelites to the Promised Land?

Yes, he would, and yes, he did! Every woman we've studied had one thing in common. Even though their lives were far from perfect, they believed in God and wanted to please him.

If you are striving to please God, no matter how messed up your life is, God can and will use you!

A thought to bloom by
Rahab's life was a mess, but God used her anyway in a mighty way.

A verse to bloom by

But thank God! He gives us victory over sin and death through our Lord Jesus Christ.

1 Corinthians 15:57

A prayer to bloom by

Abba, sometimes I don't feel worthy of your love. I've done and said things I'm ashamed of. But then I remember you've given us victory over sin and death. Your Word tells us your grace covers a multitude of sins. Thank you for reminding me to look to your Word for the truth and not to lean on my feelings. In Jesus' name, amen.

APPLICATION QUESTIONS:

· Have you ever messed up so badly that you thought you couldn't be used by God?

· Did you discover that God could use you anyway?

· What happened as a result?

CHAPTER EIGHT

KEEP ON BLOOMING

Even When You Must Wait

" Father, how could you?" Tears flowed from Rachel's red-rimmed eyes down her cheeks. "Jacob worked seven years for me and now you've tricked him. I will never forgive you for this."

> *So Laban invited everyone in the neighborhood and prepared a wedding feast. But that night, when it was dark, Laban took Leah to Jacob, and he slept with her. But when Jacob woke up in the morning – it was Leah! "What have you done to me?" Jacob raged at Laban. "I worked seven years for Rachel! Why have you tricked me?"*
>
> *Genesis 29:22-25*

During the next seven years, I took care of Niki and Dad, mostly by myself.

Shortly after I moved in with Dad, God brought a man into my life that would change it in a way I never thought possible. Travis and I met at a Christian singles group. We started dating after a few months. He was seven years older than me, but his children were younger than mine. His son was still in college and his daughter had just turned thirteen. By this time, I was leery of a relationship. The only examples of men I had to go by were Dad and Dallas. To say the least, my opinion of men was not very good.

But as time went on, and Travis and I continued to date, I saw that he was the real thing. He treated me with respect and valued my opinions. He even allowed me to have my own opinions – something I'd never experienced. He treated my girls like his own, and he understood the responsibility I had taking care of Niki and Dad.

He was the wind beneath my wings when it came to my writing. In fact, my first professional project was born from a dare Travis offered me. We had gone out to eat at a restaurant in a small town close by. The restaurant, located in a beautiful old building, was chock full of history. Travis, being an architect, noticed the quality of the building right away. While we drove home, I suggested someone needed to write an article for a magazine we both loved, the *North Georgia Journal*. He nonchalantly said, "Why don't you?" And I nonchalantly replied, "Okay, I will." And I did just that.

I looked in one of my old magazines to see who the writers were and discovered one of the contributors lived in my town. I contacted him and asked how I should go about writing an article. He was more than gracious and mentored me through the process. I was so excited when the editor notified me he wanted to publish it. I was walking on air.

I returned to the historic restaurant to take a few more pictures and talk with the owner one more time. When I arrived, her husband greeted me with, "She isn't here. She ran off with the cook over the weekend."

Now, mind you, I thought he was kidding and started to laugh until I saw the crocodile tears roll down his cheeks. Quick! I had to think of something. I did what any good reporter would do – I sat there for two hours and listened to his sad story. By the time he finished, I had to admit, I couldn't much blame her. But, nonetheless, I went from jubilation of my first article being published to the agony of defeat. That was the first experience I had on the rollercoaster ride of writing.

But the writing bug had bitten and I wasn't giving up that easily. I decided to write another story on the Great Locomotive Chase, a story about Andrews' Raiders (a gang of Northerners lead by James A. Andrews, a Northern spy) who stole a train from the Lacy House in Kennesaw, Georgia, while the crew and passengers ate breakfast. A chase pursued. The conductor and engineer of the stolen train pursued the thieves on foot, by handcar, small engine, and finally chased them backwards with the *Texas*, a train they had commandeered in Adairsville, Georgia. All the Raiders were caught and several of them were hanged, including the leader, James A. Andrews. Not only was the article published, but it was a big hit with the readers. This was the shot in the arm I needed to keep on writing.

After writing for the magazine for a couple of years, in 2002 I decided I wanted to write a novel.

Now, I admit, it proved a challenge to say the least. I'd write a paragraph, then Dad would call me from the other end of the house. I'd jump up, go see what he needed, come back, write another paragraph, then Niki would have to go to the bathroom. I'd jump up and go tend to her needs. Believe it or not, I eventually finished the first draft of my first cozy mystery, *Death in Dahlonega,* and then managed to get halfway through my next novel, *Murder in Marietta.*

As often happens, life got in the way, and I had to put away my writing for several years. Dad had endured a hip replacement, surgery for a tumor behind his ear, and carpal tunnel surgery on both hands. It had come to the point where I couldn't care for him and Niki by myself. Some tough decisions had to be made. After almost eight years of caring for them both, Dad moved into assisted living. I was still responsible for his overall care, but didn't have the physical duties. Dad lived in his apartment for almost a year until he succumbed to pneumonia.

Shortly after Dad died, Niki was involved in a horrific accident. Another curve in the road that almost made me wreck!

Then Jacob hurried on, finally arriving in the land of the east. He saw a well in the distance. Three flocks of sheep and goats lay in an open field beside it, waiting to be watered. But a heavy stone covered the mouth of the well.

Genesis 29: 1-2

Jacob went over to the shepherds and asked, "Where are you from, my friends?"

"We are from Haran," they answered.

"Do you know a man there named Laban, the grand-son of Nahor?" he asked.

"Yes, we do," they replied.

"Is he doing well?" Jacob asked.

"Yes, he's very well," they answered. "Look, here come his daughter Rachel with the flock now."

Genesis 29:4-6

Cupid's arrow penetrated Jacob's heart as the beautiful young maiden walked toward him. But that was just the beginning of what would become Jacob's turbulent life.

He was on the lam from his brother Esau. Remember, Jacob dressed like Esau and went into their father Isaac's tent and received the blessing that was rightfully Esau's. At that point in his life Isaac couldn't see past the nose on his face, and Jacob and his mother, Rebekah, took advantage of Isaac's failing sight and planned the devious stunt. They went so far as to put goatskins on Jacob's arms so he would feel hairy like Esau when Isaac touched him.

Esau was none too happy about it, and he was much bigger and stronger than Jacob; he wasn't waiting around to see what Esau would do to him. So, he set off to visit his mother's brother, Laban. He ended up at the same well where Abraham's servant found Rebekah and asked her to be Isaac's wife. Now Jacob, Isaac's son and Abraham's grandson, would also find his wife at the same well.

Jacob was still talking with them when Rachel arrived with her father's flock, for she was a shepherd. And because Rachel was his cousin – the daughter of Laban, his mother's brother – and because the sheep and goats belonged to his uncle Laban, Jacob went over to the well and moved the stone from its mouth and watered his uncle's flock. Then Jacob kissed Rachel, and he wept aloud. He explained to Rachel that he was her cousin on her father's side – the son of her aunt Rebekah. So, Rachel quickly ran and told her father, Laban.

As soon as Laban heard that his nephew Jacob had arrived, he ran out to meet him. He embraced and kissed him and brought him home. When Jacob had told him his story, Laban exclaimed, "You really are my own flesh and blood!"

Genesis 29:9-14

Jacob had traveled many miles and had never met his Uncle Laban, so he had no idea if his circumstances would be better than when he left home. When he saw Rachel at the well he didn't hesitate to remove the rock from the mouth of the well put there to keep the water clean. After he saw that she had watered her flock, he gave her a kiss. His heart had already been stolen by this beautiful girl - his cousin. The Bible says he "wept aloud," I'd wager to say he was happy about something.

Things seemed to be going well for Jacob. He found his family and his future bride all in one day. I wouldn't put too much credence in that first day, though.

Even though this could have been a kiss of salutation, Rachel was so excited she ran home and told her father who she had met at the well. Laban also joined in on the excitement of seeing his nephew and catching up on how his family had been doing.

Laban was probably given the short version – you know, the one where Jacob leaves out the part about deceiving his father and stealing Esau's birthright.

> *Now Laban had two daughters. The older daughter was named Leah, and the younger one was Rachel. There was no sparkle in Leah's eyes, but Rachel had a beautiful figure and a lovely face. Since Jacob was in love with Rachel, he told her father, "I'll work for you for seven years if you'll give me Rachel, your younger daughter, as my wife."*
>
> *Genesis 29:16-18*

Wow – Rachel must have been a looker! Jacob just promised Laban seven years of labor to gain her hand in marriage. I haven't figured out why so many of the women in the bible are described as beautiful – maybe God sees us all as beautiful. It doesn't say much about Leah's looks, but it does insinuate she may have had a problem with her eyesight, maybe indicating poor vision. Jacob gladly worked his seven years for Rachel's hand. But the trick he played on Isaac and Esau came back to haunt him.

> *Finally, the time came for him to marry her, "I have fulfilled my agreement," Jacob said to Laban. "Now give me my wife so I can sleep with her."*
>
> *So, Laban invited everyone in the neighborhood and prepared a wedding feast. But that night, when it was dark, Laban took Leah to Jacob, and he slept with her.*
>
> *But when Jacob woke up in the morning – it was Leah! "What have you done to me?" Jacob raged at Laban. "I worked seven years for Rachel! Why have you tricked me?"*

"It is not our custom here to marry off a younger daughter ahead of the firstborn," Laban replied. "But wait until the bridal week is over, then we'll give you Rachel, too – provided you promise to work another seven years for me." So Jacob agreed to work another seven years.

Genesis 29:21-28

It must have been quite the shock when Jacob woke up in the morning only to find Leah in his bed! And he wasn't a happy camper. It doesn't mean he had anything against Leah, but the agreement to work seven years was for Rachel. It's easy to imagine how angry Jacob must have been with Laban.

And what a flimsy excuse he gave Jacob for switching them on the wedding night. "It is not our custom here to marry off a younger daughter ahead of the firstborn," Laban said.

"Well thank you very much for telling me that ahead of time, Laban."

If you're reading this story for the first time, I'm sure your sympathies would go out to Jacob. But remember, seven years before he had tricked his father, Isaac, into believing he was Esau so he could receive the blessing that rightfully belonged to Esau. I wonder if Jacob put two and two together. Did he think about how angry and hurt Esau felt when he tricked him? Was he sorry? We don't know, but I have a strong feeling his misdeed came to mind once or twice during this time.

I'm sad to say, this story triggered thoughts of many times I may have hurt someone, but when the same thing was done to me I played the old righteous indignation card.

Unfortunately, sometimes we must learn the hard way about hurting others, like Jacob did.

But this is a love story, and Jacob loved Rachel enough to agree to work another seven years for her hand in marriage. He got a whole lot more than he bargained for. Now he had two wives, and they were sisters to boot. You better believe sibling rivalry played into this story.

When the Lord saw that Leah was unloved, he enabled her to have children, but Rachel could not conceive. So Leah became pregnant and gave birth to a son. She named him Reuben, for she said, "The Lord has noticed my misery, and now my husband will love me."

She soon became pregnant again and gave birth to another son. She named him Simeon, for she said, "The Lord heard I was unloved and has given me another son."

Then she became pregnant a third time and gave birth to another son. She named him Levi, for she said, "Surely this time my husband will feel affection for me, since I have given him three sons!"

Once again Leah became pregnant and gave birth to another son. She named him Judah, for she said, "Now I will praise the Lord!" And then she stopped having children.

Genesis 29:31-35

It seems Jacob took out his anger on Leah, even though she did the bidding of her father. She continued to give Jacob sons, but he continued to withhold his affection from her. How many women have said the same thing in a marriage that wasn't at its best, "Oh, if only I could have a baby. Then he would love me." But it doesn't work that way. A baby can put more stress on the marriage, as was the case in this one.

When Rachel saw that she wasn't having children for Jacob, she became jealous of her sister. She pleaded with Jacob, "Give me children, or I'll die!"

Then Jacob became furious with Rachel. "Am I God?" he asked. "He's the one who has kept you from having children."

Then Rachel told him, "Take my maid, Bilhah, and sleep with her. She will bear children for me, and through her I can have a family, too." So Rachel gave her servant, Bilhah, to Jacob as a wife, and he slept with her. Bilhah, became pregnant and presented him with a son. Rachel named him Dan, for she said, "God has vindicated me! He has heard my request and given me a son. Then Bilhah became pregnant again and gave Jacob a second son. Rachel named him Naphtali, for she said, "I have struggled hard with my sister, and I'm winning."

Genesis 30:1-8

After Rachel blamed Jacob for her being childless, he might have rethought those fourteen years. Rachel threw a temper tantrum. *Leah has children and I don't have any. I want children, too!*

Boy does that hit home. How many times have I seen others with something I'd like and have been overcome with the green-eyed monster, jealousy. I'm ashamed to say more than once.

But sibling rivalry has been normal from the beginning of time – think about Cain and Abel. And this was exactly what happened between Rachel and Leah. Rachel was so desperate, she gave her servant, Bilhah, to Jacob to bear children for her. Phew! Jacob was a busy man. He was caught between a rock and a hard place, or I should say between Rachel and Leah.

And that's made obvious when Rachel bragged, "Ha! Ha! I'll show Leah who's the winner in this game!"

Meanwhile, Leah realized that she wasn't getting pregnant anymore, so she took her servant, Zilpah, and gave her to Jacob as a wife. Soon Zilpah presented him with a son. Leah named him Gad, for she said, "How fortunate I am!" Then Zilpah gave Jacob a second son. And Leah name him Asher, for she said, "What joy is mine! Now the other women will celebrate with me."

Genesis 30:9-13

The race was on! Rachel was pulling up beside Leah, but Leah's taken off again!

Leah was not immune from this rivalry. When she didn't have more children fast enough, she gave Jacob her servant, Zilpah to bear more children for her. This was the custom of that time – if a wife couldn't bear children, then they could offer their servant to have children for them. I can only imagine how hard it must have been for these women to be used as a surrogate for their mistress, with no say in the matter. Then the mistress claimed the child as hers. Sometimes the Old Testament ways are hard to understand, and I won't attempt to explain them here.

But the rivalry never stopped until the day Rachel died.

One day during the wheat harvest, Reuben found some mandrakes growing in a field and brought them to his mother, Leah. Rachel begged Leah, "Please give me some of your son's mandrakes."

But Leah angrily replied, "Wasn't it enough that you stole my husband? Now will you steal my son's mandrakes, too?"

Rachel answered, "I will let Jacob sleep with you tonight if you give me some of the mandrakes."

Genesis 30:14-15

Well, well, well, now Rachel is begging Leah for some of her mandrakes. Mandrakes, according to the book *Hebrew Marriage*:

From the most ancient time, aphrodisiac virtues have been ascribed to the mandrake, which was therefore supposed to cure barrenness, and it is now known that the root, when eaten, would have the effect of relaxing the womb.

All the Women of the Bible

Leah wasn't in the sharing mood. "Huh, you stole my husband, why should I share with you?"

Rachel stooped to bribing, "If you give me some, I'll let Jacob sleep with you tonight."

That was good enough for Leah and she shared some of the mandrakes with Rachel.

So that evening, as Jacob was coming home from the fields, Leah went out to meet him. "You must come and sleep with me tonight!" she said. I have paid for you some mandrakes that my son found. So that night he slept with Leah. And God answered Leah's prayers. She became pregnant again and gave birth to a fifth son for Jacob. She named him Isaachar, for she said, "God has rewarded me for giving my servant to my husband as a wife." Then Leah became pregnant again and gave birth to a sixth son for Jacob. She named him Zebulun, for she said, "God has given me a good reward. Now my husband will treat me with respect, for I have given him six sons. Later she gave birth to a daughter and named her Dinah.

Genesis 30:16-21

Leah was a regular baby machine. She gave Jacob many sons and his only daughter, Dinah. This didn't help the spat between her and Rachel. But God was about to grant Rachel her wish.

Then God remembered Rachel's plight and answered her prayers by enabling her to have children. She became pregnant and gave birth to a son. "God has removed my disgrace," she said. And she named him Joseph, for she said, "May the Lord add yet another son to my family."

Genesis 30:22-24

God finally granted Rachel's one desire – children of her own. And Joseph was no ordinary son. He would become the family's savior during the famine of Egypt and Canaan.

After Jacob worked off the debt to Laban, he decided he wanted to return to his homeland. He was a wealthy man by this time. Jacob called his wives together and asked them what they thought. Rachel and Leah finally agreed on something. They agreed they needed to get away from their father and start a fresh life.

Only one thing marred their plan. They conveniently forgot to tell Laban they were going. So Laban and his men followed them until they caught up with Jacob and his daughters. After Jacob explained all the hard work he'd done for him over the years, Laban made a peace treaty with Jacob and they continued their journey.

> *Leaving Bethel, Jacob and his clan moved on toward Ephrath. But Rachel went into labor while they were still some distance away. Her labor pains were intense. After a very hard delivery, the midwife finally exclaimed, "Don't be afraid – you have another son!"*
>
> *Rachel was about to die, but with her last breath she named him Ben-oni (which means son of sorrow). The baby's father, however, called him Benjamin (which means the son of my right hand). So Rachel died and was buried on the way to Ephrath (that is Bethlehem). Jacob set up a stone monument over Rachel's grave, and it can be see there to this day.*
>
> *Genesis 35:16-20*

It's ironic that Rachel would say, "Give me children, or I'll die!" and that she died giving birth to one of those children she so desperately wanted. But God can take situations that we think are the darkest in our lives and turn them around. Rachel waited and waited to have children while Leah popped them out right and left. She didn't understand what she'd done to become barren.

That's what happens so many times in our lives. We only see underneath the quilt, where it has been pieced together. With strings hanging here and there it looks like a hodge-podge of scraps, instead of what it is: a beautiful work of art – the finished piece that God sees.

The quilter must wait until the quilt is finished before she can see the total design. The beginning quilter might think, "Oh, look at those beautiful quilts. I wish mine looked like that." And someday it will, it just takes time. We might see other families who seem to have it all: money, things, nice house, great marriage. But we can't see on the inside of that family. We don't really know what their lives are like. Remember, during our times of trials we are being molded and shaped to be our best.

A thought to bloom by
Rachel had to wait on her dreams for God's perfect timing.

A verse to bloom by
Wait patiently for the Lord. Be brave and courageous. Yes, wait patiently for the Lord.

Psalm 27:14

A prayer to bloom by
Abba, I admit sometimes I'm not very patient. I get discouraged if my prayers aren't answered right away. If they are not answered in my timing then I think they won't be answered. Please forgive my impatience and fill me with the ability to wait on you. In Jesus' name, amen.

APPLICATION QUESTIONS:

· What are you waiting for?

· What helpful things can you do while you wait?

CHAPTER NINE

KEEP ON BLOOMING

Even When You Don't Understand Why God Permitted Your Pain

She ignored the stares and whispers as she watched over her sons' bodies. "Is she crazy?" many asked as they passed by.

"Why does she sit day after day on that rock? Does she plan on sitting there forever?" People shook their heads as they passed by and stared.

It was going on five months now, and she still guarded her sons. "Don't they understand? Wouldn't they do the same," Rizpah wondered? (2 Samuel 21:10).

For over a year, Niki went to respite on the weekends at a group home so I could get much-needed rest. I'd told them several times she couldn't be left alone, even showing them a picture of Niki with a broken arm. She was a whiz at wheeling her chair, but didn't understand safety issues. Kind of like a toddler – they're able to walk, but don't understand they can fall off something.

Lo and behold, what did they do? Left her alone. The caregiver had gone outside with the other clients and left Niki in the house. Niki decided she wanted to go outside, too, so she opened the door, and rolled down concrete steps onto a concrete landing. Needless to say, she sustained substantial injuries. She would require stitches in her head and had scrapes and bruises over her body.

But this wasn't the worst of her injuries. She healed from these, but began having other problems. Over the next several months it became apparent something was very wrong. The fall had damaged her ventricular shunt, a drainage system located in her brain used to drain off excess fluid. This shunt was the one she'd gotten when she was in Atlanta many years before.

Over the next year, her injury resulted in two surgeries to replace the shunt, plus the endurance of intense therapy to try to get her back to where she was before the accident. Niki was a trooper through all of this, just like always.

Not long after the surgeries, I knew my body had reached a point where I wasn't able to care for Niki by myself any longer. My pain had become unbearable, and depression was a frequent companion.

I began to search for ways to get help with Niki. By this time, Travis and I had been dating for almost eight years. We were committed to each other and wanted to marry. His children were older now, but I didn't feel I could be the wife I wanted to be while devoting the time I needed to care for Niki. He never pressured me or made me feel guilty about my decision to keep Niki at home.

Through the years there were many times I looked at other people and thought, "Oh, they must have a wonderful life." I admit I was envious of others and wished I had a life free of challenges. I know now that no one gets a free pass in this life. Everyone will encounter challenges and disappointments as long as they are breathing on this earth.

During this time, I had gone to our local car wash to run my car through. As I sat in the lobby, the owner saw me on my computer. She asked if I was "working." I replied, "No." And she looked me in the eyes and said, "Oh, I wish I had it that easy."

Little did she know my heart was breaking, as well as my back. I'd reached a point, or age, in my life where I wasn't afraid to speak my feelings. I told her about Niki and the possibility of not being able to care for her. The look on her face said it all. She had made an assumption and she was now sorry. She sputtered an apology and I even got a free car wash out of the deal. I really can't fault her, because I had thought the same thing many times about other people. I try to think twice before I make assumptions now.

I discovered a program for adult children with disabilities that would provide in-home care giving, allowing Niki to stay at home with me. We started off with eight hours a day. The first angel to come to us was Patricia. She stayed as our daytime caregiver for the seven years we were in the program. With Patricia helping, it was the first time I could just hop in the car and make a run to the store if I needed to. And I seemed to find reasons to go to the store quite often.

I hadn't experienced that kind of freedom since Niki became sick.

The relief during the day was great, but it wasn't enough. I still got up many times during the night to take Niki to the bathroom or tend to her other needs. I continued to physically work with her at night and all weekend (she never returned to respite after the fall) by myself.

I contacted the government agency and requested more help. Niki required a high level of assistance, called an exceptional rate. I was told there was a freeze on providing caregivers for her level. I begged, pleaded and called everybody I knew to no avail. I knew if I didn't get help soon I'd be in deep trouble, or more aptly put, "in deep doo-doo!"

There is no greater grief than that of a mother over the death of her children, and there is no end to what she will do for them. Rizpah was one of King Saul's concubines, and they had two sons together, Mephibosheth and Armoni.

> *"What happened?" David demanded. "Tell me how the battle went."*
>
> *The man replied, "Our entire army fled from the battle. Many of the men are dead, and Saul and his son Jonathan are also dead."*
>
> *"How do you know Saul and Jonathan are dead?" David demanded of the young man.*
>
> *The man answered, "I happened to be on Mount Gilboa, and there was Saul leaning on his spear with the enemy chariots and charioteers closing in on him. When*

he turned and saw me, he cried out for me to come to him. 'How can I help?' I asked him.

"He responded, 'Who are you?'

"'I am an Amalekite,' I told him.

"Then he begged me, 'Come over here and put me out of my misery, for I am in terrible pain and want to die.'

"So I killed him," the Amalekite told David, "for I knew he couldn't live. Then I took his crown and his armband, and I have brought them here to you, my lord."

David and his men tore their clothes in sorrow when they heard the news.

2 Samuel 1:4-11

King Saul was the first king to rule over all the tribes of Israel, and David and Saul had a love-hate relationship. Rizpah, King Saul's concubine, first suffered through the death of King Saul and later, the gruesome death of her two sons.

As the war between the house of Saul and the house of David went on, Abner became a powerful leader among those loyal to Saul. One day Ishbosheth, Saul's son, accused Abner of sleeping with one of his father's concubines, a woman named Rizpah, daughter of Aiah.

Abner was furious. "Am I some Judean dog to be kicked around like this?" he shouted. "After all I have done for you and your father, Saul, and his family and friends by not handing you over to David, is this my reward – that you find fault with me about this woman?"

2 Samuel 3:7-8

Rizpah was used as a political tool, not as a woman who had feelings and desires of her own. After Saul's death, Abner and Ishbosheth contended over Rizpah, hoping any offspring from her might lead them to the throne. Abner took her for his concubine considering that if he could have a son with Rizpah, then he would have a remote claim to the throne.

> *There was a famine during David's reign that lasted for three years, so David asked the Lord about it. And the Lord said, "The famine has come because Saul and his family are guilty of murdering the Gibeonites."*
>
> *So the king summoned the Gibeonites... David asked them, "What can I do for you? How can I make amends so that you will bless the Lord's people again?"*
>
> *They then replied, "It was Saul who planned to destroy us, to keep us from having any place at all in the territory of Israel. So let seven of Saul's sons be handed over to us, and we will execute them before the Lord at Gibeon, on the mountain of the Lord."*
>
> *"All right," the king said, "I will do it." The king spared Johnathan's son Mephibosheth, who was Saul's grandson, because of the oath David and Jonathan had sworn before the Lord. But he gave them Saul's two sons Armoni and Mephibosheth, whose mother was Rizpah daughter of Aiah.*
>
> *2 Samuel 21:1-8*

Soon after Saul's death, Israel was struck with a famine. King David asked God why they were being punished. God replied the famine was a result of King Saul's attempt to eradicate the Gibeonite people.

King David asked the Gibeonites what he could do to reverse the situation. They answered that David must hand over Saul's heirs to be tortured and killed. The heirs included Rizpah's two sons, as well as the five sons of Saul's daughter.

I can hear Rizpah crying out to the Lord, "Why? Why my sons? This is too much for me to bear. I don't understand."

Since the beginning of time, tragedies have happened that humans do not have the capacity to understand. Like Rizpah, I don't understand why Niki has gone through so much, but I know God can take our heartaches and make something beautiful from them.

> *Then Rizpah daughter of Aiah, the mother of two of the men, spread burlap on a rock and stayed there the entire harvest season. She prevented the scavenger birds from tearing at their bodies during the day and stopped the wild animals from eating them at night.*
>
> *2 Samuel 21:10*

Rizpah's sons were left to rot where they lay after being killed. She covered them the best she could and spread sackcloth over a nearby rock where she guarded the bodies from vultures during the day and beasts of prey at night. Her purple raiment of royalty had been exchanged for sackcloth. She sat like this for five months until David heard of her vigil.

> *Then the king ordered that they bury the bones in the tomb of Kish, Saul's father, at the town of Zela in the land of Benjamin. After that, God ended the famine in the land.*
>
> *2 Samuel 21:14*

King David ordered a proper burial of her sons, as well as Saul and his son, Jonathan, who had never been buried. After the burials, the famine was lifted.

> Rizpah's desires, wishes, and welfare were never foremost in the minds of Abner, Ishbosheth, or David. She was a tool to the crown and an avenue to the throne. Yet she shows strength in adversity by persevering for the burial of her dead son's bodies. Her use as a bargaining chip is certainly demeaning, but she emerges a woman of honor, as opposed to those who sought to use her as an object rather than relate to her as a person.
>
> Women in the Bible for Dummies

A thought to bloom by

Rizpah lived through terrible pain and discovered that some questions won't be answered until heaven.

A verse to bloom by

Trust in the Lord with all your heart; do not depend on your own understanding. Seek his will in all you do, and he will show you which path to take.

Proverbs 3:5-6

A prayer to bloom by

Precious Abba, please take this pain from me and heal my broken heart. I need you, Abba. At times, the pain is so deep I can hardly breathe. I don't understand why we must go through the dark times, but I know, without a doubt, you hold me in your hands during that time. Even Jesus had to go through dark times, and when he did he turned to you for strength and comfort. Help me to remember to turn to you for my comfort and strength during dark days. In Jesus' name, amen.

APPLICATION QUESTIONS:

· Is there a question that you've been asking God that he hasn't answered?

· What are some things you can do to trust him even though you don't understand?

CHAPTER TEN

KEEP ON BLOOMING

Even When You're Ashamed of Something You Did

The lone woman stealthily searched her surroundings as she approached Jacob's well. She knew too well the sting of gossip from the local women. Why else would she be going to the well at the hottest time of day?

> *Eventually he came to the Samaritan village of Sychar, near the field that Jacob gave to his son Joseph. Jacobs well was there; and Jesus, tired from the long walk, sat wearily beside the well at noontime.*
>
> John 4:5-6

It was high noon and the sun blazed down with intensity. Sweat beaded on her forehead as she trudged along the worn path, and dust covered her sandaled feet with every step she took. Most of the women went to the well in the early morning or late afternoon to avoid the hot sun. But the Samaritan woman endured the sun so she wouldn't have to endure pointing fingers and wagging tongues. But what she didn't expect to see was a man sitting at the well.

My pain level had become unbearable and indescribable. Every part of my body ached and I couldn't stand for anyone to touch me. The pain and the depression had become a vicious cycle. One exacerbated the other and I was on a downward spiral. I wound up in the hospital for pain management and treatment for the depression. I'd come to a point in my life where I didn't care if I lived or not – I just needed relief.

An angel, in the form of a hospital social worker, saved me. She asked if there was anything she could do. I spilled my heart out and told her about Niki. I had one contact I hadn't called yet, and she offered to call him for me. She talked with him a minute then put me on the phone. We had finally reached the right person. He said he'd call me right back. Within five minutes, he had news that we had the funding we needed for Niki's extra help. By the time I went home, I had someone to help with the night shift. Unfortunately, I've learned that too many times it takes something as serious as a hospital stay to light the fire under government agencies.

I was thrilled to have the help with Niki and have her at home with me. But having someone in your home seven days a week, twenty-four hours a day was far from fun. It was downright stressful, and afforded me little privacy. But we began to get used to our new routine.

One day, I was reading a novel by Margaret Daley. When I finished, I *knew* that was how I wanted to write my books. I went to Margaret's website and discovered what she wrote was called "Christian Fiction." What? I'd never even heard of Christian Fiction. I saw on the site that she belonged to an on-line Christian writing group, called American Christian Fiction Writers.

I don't even remember how I came to have Margaret's book, but I felt God's hand guiding me. I took *Death in Dahlonega* from the shelf and blew off the dust. It took the next few years of learning the craft of writing, and then rewriting *Death in Dahlonega,* before I thought it was good enough for submission. I had just turned fifty-seven when my first book was published.

Is it possible to put the past behind you and move on to greater things? Just ask the Samaritan woman at the well.

I developed a phrase I quote to my writing classes, "Passion + Perseverance = Publication." It's the writers who don't give up that become published authors. Every author has a story to tell about rejections they received. One such story is Debbie Macomber's. If you don't know who she is – you should, so look her up.

Debbie told this story at a conference where she was the keynote speaker. When she first started writing she submitted a manuscript in a contest at a writer's conference.

Someone from the conference called and asked if she would be there for the awards ceremony. Of course, she'd be there! Debbie was so excited she could hardly wait until the awards were handed out. But when her name was called, instead of receiving the coveted prize, her manuscript was used as an example of how not to write.

I can't even begin to imagine the pain and embarrassment she felt. Most people would have sworn off writing after that. Not Debbie. Her passion was great, and so she went to the person who had humiliated her and asked how she could do a better job. She wanted to write!

The editor told her she shouldn't be writing. Double whammy! Like anybody with a heart, Debbie went home devastated. She put the manuscript away and didn't touch it for six months. But Debbie's passion and perseverance were greater than her disappointment. She wasn't letting one person destroy her dreams. She reworked the manuscript. It was accepted by a well-known publishing house, and the rest is history. Debbie now has over 150 published books, Hallmark movies, and a Hallmark Channel series. Don't ever let someone steal your dream!

Soon a Samaritan woman came to draw water, and Jesus said to her. "Please give me a drink." He was alone at the time because his disciples had gone into the village to buy some food.

John 4:7-8

Startled, she looked around to see if this man was talking to someone else. Nope, nobody there but her. This man was a Jew, and everybody knew a Jew wouldn't go out of their way to speak to the hated mixed race of the Samaritans. Second, she was a woman, and they were alone; a respectable Jew wouldn't be speaking to a Samaritan woman under those circum-stances. But he did!

> *The woman was surprised, for Jews refuse to have any-thing to do with Samaritans. She said to Jesus, "You are a Jew, and I am a Samaritan woman. Why are you asking me for a drink?"*
>
> John 4:9

I don't think it's coincidental that Jesus approached the well the same time the woman came to draw water. He chose a path that led right through Samaria, a place most Jews would have avoided. But not Jesus. He had a plan for this woman. Little did she know the conversation with this Jewish man would change her life forever.

> *Jesus replied, "If you only knew the gift God has for you and who you are speaking to, you would ask me, and I would give you living water."*
> *"But sir, you don't have a rope or a bucket," she said, "and this well is very deep. Where would you get this living water? And besides, do you think you're greater than our ancestor Jacob, who gave us this well? How can you offer better water than he and his sons and his animals enjoyed?"*
>
> John 4:10-12

She didn't understand the gift Jesus talked about. She thought he was talking about the water in Jacob's well, which came mostly from rainwater and dew, not the best drinking water to be found. But thinking he was talking about the actual water, she took offense at his comments and challenged him on the quality of their ancestor's water. There's been a time or two in my life I've misunderstood what someone said and jumped the gun and became defensive.

> *Jesus replied, "Anyone who drinks this water will soon become thirsty again. But those who drink the water I give them will never be thirsty again. It becomes a fresh, bubbling spring within them, giving them eternal life."*
>
> *"Please sir," the woman said, "give me this water! Then I'll never be thirsty again, and I won't have to come here to get the water."*
>
> John 4:13-14

She's still thinking in human terms. Water is essential to our very life. A week without water and we're doomed. She had no choice but to come to the well for water to sustain her life. It wasn't so much she wouldn't be physically thirsty again, as much as she would never have to endure the agony of judgment from the other women who came to the well to fill their jugs. "All right! I want some of this water. Bring it on!" But Jesus shifted the conversation and threw her for a loop.

> *"Go and get your husband," Jesus told her.*
> *"I don't have a husband," the woman replied.*
> *Jesus said, "You're right! You don't have a husband – for you have had five husbands, and you aren't even married to the man you're living with now. You certainly spoke the truth!"*
>
> John 4:16-18

Why did Jesus change the subject here and point out her faults? She certainly wasn't getting the picture Jesus tried to paint for her with words – living water, everlasting life. He wasn't trying to shame her by pointing out her faults. He was letting her know, despite her shortcomings, there was still hope for this gift of eternal life he was trying to give her. I get chills thinking about this. Jesus loved this woman enough that he went out of his way to travel a path leading him to her so he could offer her what he offers each of us. The gift of eternal life.

> *"Sir," the woman said, "you must be a prophet. So tell me, why is it that you Jews insist that Jerusalem is the only place to worship, while we Samaritans claim it is here at Mount Gerizim, where our ancestors worshiped?"*
> John 4:19-20

She's beginning to see that the conversation with this man is different than anything she has experienced before. He knew way too much about her and she felt uncomfortable. Was this man going to judge her like everyone else? The sweat ran down her forehead; she swiped at it with the back of her hand. She had to think fast on her feet – and she did. What did she do to get out of this uncomfortable situation? Maybe she'd used this tactic in the past and it had worked, so she tried it again. She changed the subject. She took the focus off herself and put it back on Jesus. That's okay, because he just used it as a segue to further his lesson.

> *Jesus replied, "Believe me, dear woman, the time is coming when it will no longer matter whether you worship the*

Father on this mountain or in Jerusalem. You Samaritans know very little about the one you worship, while we Jews know all about him, for salvation comes through the Jews. But the time is coming – indeed it's here now – when true worshipers will worship the Father in spirit and in truth. The Father is looking for those who will worship him that way. For God is Spirit, so those who worship him must worship in spirit and in truth."

The woman said, "I know the Messiah is coming – the one who is called Christ. When he comes, he will explain everything to us."

Then Jesus told her, "I Am the Messiah!"

John 4:21-26

Whoa, when she changed the subject to take the heat off herself, she didn't expect the conversation to go in that direction. He took her very words and used them to teach her. There would come a time when it didn't matter *where* you worshiped – but *who* you worshiped. She wanted him to know she was knowledgeable about this Savior – and when he came he'd be the ultimate authority on the subject. I can't imagine what must have gone through her mind when Jesus told her "I Am the Messiah!" She probably stood, mouth open, staring at this man who claimed to be the Savior.

Just then his disciples came back. They were shocked to find him talking to a woman, but none of them had the nerve to ask, "What do you want with her?" or "Why are you talking to her?"

John 4:27

But she didn't have time to answer because the disciples returned. We're left to wonder who was more shocked. The disciples who saw Jesus talking not only to a woman, but a Samaritan, or the woman who just learned this man she'd been debating religion with was the Messiah?

> *The woman left her water jar beside the well and ran back to the village, telling everyone, "Come and see a man who told me everything I ever did! Could he possibly be the Messiah?" So the people came streaming from the village to see him.*
>
> John 4:28-30

Could this possibly be the same woman who came to the well at the hottest time of the day to avoid people? She was so excited by the news Jesus had just shared, she left her water jug at the well and took off running to the village, her thirst now forgotten. Her confidence just shot up one hundred percent.

> *Meanwhile, the disciples were urging Jesus, "Rabbi, eat something."*
>
> *But Jesus replied, "I have a kind of food you know nothing about."*
>
> *"Did someone bring him food while we were gone?" the disciples asked each other.*
>
> *Then Jesus explained: "My nourishment comes from doing the will of God, who sent me, and from finishing his work. You know the saying 'Four months between planting and harvest.' But I say, wake up and look around. The fields are already ripe for harvest. The harvesters are paid good wages, and the fruit they harvest is people*

brought to eternal life. What joy awaits both the planter and the harvester alike! You know the saying, 'One plants and another harvests.' And it's true. I sent you to harvest where you didn't plant; others had already done the work, and now you will get to gather the harvest."

John 4:31-38

The disciples focused on Jesus eating something instead of on the woman he was talking to, but he wasn't about to miss this golden opportunity to teach his faithful followers. He compared the physical body to the Spiritual body. Both need to be fed, but the amazing thing about spiritual food is that you can satisfy that hunger not only by studying, praying and attending services, but by giving. Serving others can satisfy spiritual hunger. How much was taught that day at the well, because of one woman's need to know about God's love for her.

Many Samaritans from the village believed in Jesus because the woman had said, "He told me everything I ever did!" When they came out to see him, they begged him to stay in their village. So he stayed for two days, long enough for many more to hear his message and believe. Then they said to the woman, "Now we believe, not just because of what you told us, but because we have heard him ourselves. Now we know that he is indeed the Savior of the world."

John 4:39-42

Knowing that the Savior cared about her gave this woman a courage and self-esteem she had probably never possessed.

He didn't focus on her shortcomings; he focused on her needs. She went from zero self-esteem to boldly announcing Jesus "had told her everything I ever did!" to anyone who would listen. She urged the people to come with her and see for themselves. And come they did. There were so many they pleaded with Jesus to stay longer. Surely, they wanted to tell their family and friends to come see this Jesus, the Messiah.

She didn't wait until she was "perfect" to share the gospel. Jesus had just pointed out her sin, not to shame her, but to let her know it wasn't too late for her to change. Think about it. Who wants to listen to someone who's self-righteous? Aren't we more apt to listen to someone who has experienced the pitfalls and heartaches of life and come through on the other side with their faith stronger for it? If you ever feel "not good enough," just remember the Samaritan woman at the well.

A thought to bloom by
The Samaritan Woman put the past behind her and moved forward.

A verse to bloom by
This means that anyone who belongs to Christ has become a new person. The old life is gone; a new life has begun!
2 Corinthians 5:17

A prayer to bloom by
Abba, we praise and worship you, the creator of our hearts and souls. Abba, I'm ashamed of things I've done in the past. I humbly come before you and ask for your

forgiveness. I thank you that because of our precious brother Jesus, who gave his life for us, we can be forgiven. Help me to remember that those sins are not only forgiven, but forgotten. Help me to remember that the past stays in the past and a new day has begun. In Jesus' name, amen.

APPLICATION QUESTIONS:

· What mistakes in your past do you need to put behind you?

· Are there any mistakes that keep you from moving ahead?

CHAPTER ELEVEN

KEEP ON BLOOMING

Even When Tempted to Take Things in Your Own Hands

"I know what the Lord told you, Abram. But I haven't had a child yet, and now I'm too old. I don't see how it can happen. Please let my servant Hagar have a child for me."

Then the Lord said to him, *"No, your servant will not be your heir, for you will have a son of your own who will be your heir"* (Genesis 15:4).

> *Now Sarai, Abram's wife had not been able to bear children for him. But she had an Egyptian servant named Hagar. So Sarai said to Abram, "The Lord has prevented me from having children. Go and sleep with my servant. Perhaps I can have children through her." And Abram agreed with Sarai's proposition.*
>
> Genesis 16:1-2

After my first book was published I continued to attend writer's conferences and began selling my book. By the next November, *Murder in Marietta* was published. I quickly discovered I enjoyed marketing as well as writing. I'd always been a people person and took to marketing like a pointer takes to hunting.

I decided I'd like to teach marketing and writing. I started by going to conferences close by so I wouldn't be away from Niki too long. God began opening doors for my writing and teaching – and I did so as often as I could.

But life's challenges continued. The stress of always having someone in my home and not being able to keep weekend staff was wearing on me. If someone didn't show up – as they often did, then I was left to care for Niki alone. Every time this happened I became overwhelmed with fear and anxiety. The agency had no one to take the place of staff who missed. And it wasn't unusual for someone to come in one day and not show up the next – they had quit. There would be at least a four-week interval before the agency could find someone else and train them.

At this point, I was taking anti-depressants as well as wearing a pain patch to function. Even through all of this, Travis and I were still dating. There were days I longed to be married, but I couldn't ask him to live in the chaos of having caregivers around the clock. I had no doubt we'd get married someday, but there were times I couldn't imagine how it would happen.

It had been many years since I'd gone to church. With everything I'd been through, I didn't feel "good enough" to go. I'd been brought up in a church where people didn't talk about the real problems that are faced by Christians. I believed if you were a *good* Christian then you wouldn't have problems. But I longed for a church family.

My brother invited me to a new church that had just started up. After attending, I knew I'd found my church family. I learned about a God that loved and used broken people for his glory - aren't we all broken in some way? This church loved and accepted you where you were in your walk and desired to help you on your journey to be more like Jesus. Travis and I have been attending for almost three years now and I've grown to know Jesus like I never thought I would.

But back to the problem of keeping caregivers. It became harder and harder to keep weekend help. Then Patricia was injured in a car accident that made it difficult for her to care for Niki. With deep regret, we lost Patricia as a caregiver. Niki and I were devastated. She had become like a second mother to Niki.

We went through several caregivers before I knew it was time for Niki to transition into a group home for adults with disabilities. She was now thirty-seven years old, and I sure wasn't getting any younger. Although I didn't have a choice, I knew this would be a good move for the future. I knew when something happened to me, Niki would already be settled in her *home*. And I'd be there to help her through the transition. God can take devastating situations and turn them around for good.

I set out to look for a new home for Niki.

Sarah experienced many events in her life before she had the baby she so desired. Like most of us she wanted a baby and wasn't willing to wait on God's timing. If our desires don't happen right away, we think they aren't going to happen at all. Sarah learned God's timing is not always our timing – something I've learned, too.

> *The Lord had said to Abram, "Leave your native country, your relatives, and your father's family, and go to the land that I will show you. I will make you into a great nation. I will bless you and make you famous, and you will be a blessing to others. I will bless those who bless you and curse those who treat you with contempt. All the families on earth will be blessed through you."*
>
> *Genesis 12:1-3*

Well, that took a little bit of faith on Abraham's part. He was seventy-five at the time – no young buck. God asked him to give up everything and strike out on an adventure to the promised land.

Sarah and Abraham became nomads traveling where God led them. They traveled until they reached the land of Canaan and set up camp there. A severe famine hit Canaan, forcing Abraham to leave and go to Egypt. Here Abraham devised a plan to trick the Pharaoh.

> *At that time a severe famine struck the land of Canaan, forcing Abram to go down to Egypt, where he lived as a foreigner. As he was approaching the border of Egypt, Abram said to his wife, Sarai, "Look, you are a very*

beautiful woman. When the Egyptians see you, they will say, 'This is his wife. Let's kill him; then we can have her!' So please tell them you are my sister. Then they will spare my life and treat me well because of their interest in you."

Genesis 12:10-13

I don't know about you, but I don't think I'd like being used as a pawn, or being passed off as my husband's sister. Although, this *was* a half-truth, as she was his half-sister. It was not unusual for half-siblings to marry during the patriarchal era.

However, the ploy worked and the Pharaoh took Sarai into his harem and gave Abraham many gifts: sheep, goats, cattle, donkeys, male and female servants, and camels. Humph, looks like Abraham got the better end of this deal.

The Lord didn't seem to think it was a good idea either. He sent plagues on Pharaoh's household until he got the hint. He summoned Abraham, "What have you done to me?" he demanded. "Why did you lie and tell me she was your sister instead of your wife? Take her and get out of here! And don't come back!"

I wonder if Abraham got an earful from Sarah, "See what your brilliant plan accomplished? You almost got us both killed. I hope you've learned your lesson."

Unfortunately, Abraham, didn't learn his lesson and pulled the same stunt again with Abimelech. But God came to Abimelech in a dream and told him Sarah was Abraham's wife and to return her to her husband. God didn't have to tell Abimelech twice. The next morning, he returned her to Abraham.

Sometime later, the Lord spoke to Abram in a vision and said to him, "Do not be afraid, Abram, for I will protect you and your reward will be great."

But Abram replied, "O Sovereign Lord, what good are all your blessings when I don't even have a son? Since you've given me no children, Eliezer or Damascus, a servant in my household, will inherit all my wealth. You have given me no descendants of my own, so one of my servants will be my heir."

Then the Lord said to him, "No, your servant will not be your heir, for you will have a son of your own who will be your heir."

Genesis 15:1-4

Abraham took his finger and shook his ear, not believing what he'd heard. "Did I hear you right, Lord?"

"Abraham, look up at the sky. See the stars filling the sky tonight? That's how many descendants you will have!"

Abraham shared the good news with Sarah. Like most people would do when they don't get what they want right away, and knowing she was not a young chick anymore, she took matters into her own hands. There would be times she regretted making that decision.

Now Sarai, Abram's wife, had not been able to bear children for him. But she had an Egyptian servant named, Hagar. So Sarai said to Abram, "The Lord has prevented me from having children. Go and sleep with my servant. Perhaps I can have children through her." And Abram agreed with Sarai's proposal.

Genesis 16:1-2

Sarah couldn't wait on God to work in her life. So, she handled it herself. I admit I've been known to do this more than once in my lifetime. During trials or challenges, it's easy to think God isn't working fast enough and we need to give him a little hand. *Surely, he could use our help.* That's what Sarah thought, so she offered Hagar to Abraham. I'm sure Abraham didn't hesitate when Sarah offered him Hagar. He'd do whatever it took to make Sarah happy.

Abraham heeded Sarah's plea and before long, Hagar was with child. But even the best laid plans don't always work like we think they will. If Sarah were here she would tell you herself.

> *So Abram had sexual relations with Hagar, and she became pregnant. But when Hagar knew she was pregnant, she began to look at her mistress, Sarai, with contempt. Then Sarai said to Abram, "This is all your fault! I put my servant into your arms, but now that she's pregnant she treats me with contempt. The Lord will show who's wrong – you or me!"*
>
> *Abram replied, "Look, she is your servant, so deal with her as you see fit." Then Sarai treated Hagar so harshly that she finally ran away.*
>
> *Genesis 16:4-6*

I laughed out loud when I read what Sarah said to Abraham, "It's all your fault!" I can just see her wagging her finger in his face.

"Listen, Sarah, she's your servant and this was your idea. Deal with her as you please." What else could poor ole Abraham say?

You'd think it would be obvious that having these family dynamics would cause friction, but Sarah was blinded by her desire to have a child.

Hagar ran away from Sarah's harsh treatment, but God instructed her to return and he'd take care of her. She returned, and Sarah treated Hagar's son, Ishmael, as her own until she gave birth to her own son, Isaac.

The Lord kept his word and did for Sarah exactly what he had promised. She became pregnant, and she gave birth to a son for Abraham in his old age. This happened at just the time God had said it would. And Abraham named their son Isaac. Eight days after Isaac was born, Abraham circumcised him as God had commanded. Abraham was 100 years old when Isaac was born.

And Sarah declared, "God has brought me laughter. All who hear about this will laugh with me. Who would have said to Abraham that Sarah would nurse a baby? Yet, I have given Abraham a son in his old age!"

Genesis 21:1-7

What is impossible with man is possible with God. Looking at her circumstances, Sarah couldn't see the outcome that wouldn't come until years later. Now she held a baby boy in her arms. She had come through so many trials and tribulations to get to the happiest time of her life. So many times, it's hard for us to see any good coming from the fire we are walking through at the time. At my darkest moments, I felt so alone and wondered where God was during those painful years. I'm so thankful I never turned my back on God. He is always with us and will take those painful times and use them for good.

And the Holy Spirit helps us in our weakness. For example, we don't know what God wants us to pray for. But the Holy Spirit prays for us with groanings that cannot be expressed in words. And the Father who knows all hearts knows what the Spirit is saying, for the Spirit pleads for us believers in harmony with God's own will. And we know that God causes everything to work together for the good of those who love God and are called according to his purpose for them.

Romans 8:26-28

A thought to bloom by

Sarah couldn't wait, and took things into her own hands, making matters worse.

Verse to bloom by

Don't worry about anything; instead, pray about everything. Tell God what you need, and thank him for all he has done.

Philippians 4:6

A prayer to bloom by

Abba, I've messed up so often. I have taken matters into my own hands and made things worse than they were before. Please fill me with the patience and understanding I need to wait on you to work in my life. Help me trust you and know that your timing isn't always my timing. In Jesus' name, amen.

APPLICATION QUESTIONS:

· Have you ever taken things in your own hands, making matters worse?

· What happened?

CHAPTER TWELVE

KEEP ON BLOOMING

Even When Your Circumstances Aren't the Way You Want Them to Be

"Lord, how long must I suffer? How long will my womb be barren? If you give me a son I will dedicate him to you." Hannah's heart was broken. Year after year she remained childless. Her arms aching to hold a baby.

> *Hannah was in deep anguish, crying bitterly as she prayed to the Lord. And she made this vow, "O Lord of Heaven's Armies, if you will look upon my sorrow and answer my prayer and give me a son, then I will give him back to you.*
>
> 1 Samuel 1:10-11

With all of Niki's medical needs, she required a special home – one for the medically fragile. They were few and far between, and finding one that was top-notch wouldn't be easy. While waiting in a doctor's office earlier in the year, I'd heard a woman talking about some new homes being built in our town for disabled adults. I asked if she had a card, and she handed me one.

Niki's support coordinator had told me about a couple of homes located approximately an hour away. After visiting, I knew right away Niki wouldn't be happy in either home – they reminded me of a medical center – not home.

One day while I was in town running errands, I saw a sign that looked familiar. It was the agency on the card I'd received earlier. I whipped my van in the driveway and rushed in to see if I could get some information. The agency director happened to be the one I talked to that day – normally it would have been the receptionist. I explained our situation and asked if their homes would be suitable for Niki. An opening in a medically fragile home had just become available and it was located about fifteen minutes from our home.

The director got in contact with Niki's support coordinator and we set up a visit. As soon as I stepped into the house and looked around I knew I'd found Niki's new "home." It would take several months before all the paperwork was completed and Niki moved in. I can't describe how hard the transition was – for both of us. Niki was a trooper, as usual. There were bumps in the road for a while, but the staff helped Niki *and me* through the transition. As I write this, Niki has been in her new home almost two years.

Her health had already begun to decline before she moved, but over the past couple of years I've seen her lose a lot of ground. It hurts my heart to see her lose what little abilities she had, but I'm thankful she was at a place that could provide her with the nursing care she needed.

Four months after Niki moved into her new home, Travis and I got married. I couldn't ask for a more caring man. Not only does he love me and my children, but he loves God. What a beautiful combination! And he has always encouraged my writing.

It's been six years since my first book was published. I now have six Christian Cozy Mysteries available. When Niki moved, it would be the first time in sixty years I didn't feel total responsibility for someone else's welfare. I now had someone to help me. I attended conferences without worrying about being called home because a staff member didn't show up or something had happened that required me to return early.

Doors began opening, and I've had many opportunities to teach and speak. There was a time when I was a young lady I thought I'd enjoy being an inspirational speaker, but I never set out to do that. I never felt "worthy" enough to speak to others about God.

Now we come to the reason I've written this book. I've learned, and want you to learn, from women in the Bible. God doesn't need us to be perfect to be used for his glory. If we wait until we're perfect, we'll be waiting till the cows come home. As you should have discovered by now, God used women right where they were in their faith journey. Some were further along than others, but that didn't matter – they were all flawed.

I look back and see that everything I went through has made me the person I am. I wouldn't be writing this book, encouraging other women if I hadn't walked through the darkness myself. My prayer is that through this study you'll come to realize that God's timing might not be our timing, but that doesn't mean our goals or ministry won't happen.

One thing I want to stress, even when you are in the darkness, you can grow. When you emerge into the light, you'll be able to offer encouragement to others.

> *All praise to God, the Father of our Lord Jesus Christ. God is our merciful Father and the source of all comfort. He comforts us in all our troubles so that we can comfort others. When they are troubled, we will be able to give them the same comfort God has given us.*
>
> *2 Corinthians 1:3-4*

Picture a clay pot broken and cracked. Flowers have found the cracks and bloomed in those broken places, making the marred pot beautiful. Remember, you too, can bloom in the broken places.

> *There was a man named Elkanah who lived in Ramah in the region of Zuph in the hill country of Ephraim. He was the son of Jeroham, son of Elihu, son of Tohu son of Zuph, of Ephraim.*
>
> *1 Samuel 1:1*

Phew, that was a mouthful. Hannah lived around the eleventh century BC, during the time Israel was ruled by Judges. She was the wife of Elkanah, a simple priest.

*Elkanah had two wives, Hannah and Peninnah. Peninnah
had children, but Hannah did not.*

1 Samuel 1:2

Hannah wasn't Elkanah's only wife. When Hannah
remained barren, Elkanah married a second wife, Peninnah.

Often, the men would marry multiple wives if one could
not conceive. This is what happened to Hannah. Even though
Elkanah loved and adored Hannah, she had no children.
Hence, the entrance of Peninnah into this family.

*Year after year it was the same – Peninnah would taunt
Hannah as they went to the Tabernacle. Each time,
Hannah would be reduced to tears and would not even eat.*

1 Samuel 1:7

Marriage can be hard between a man and wife. I can't
imagine the dynamics of having more than one wife in the
family. It didn't go well for Hannah. While she remained
barren, Peninnah was having babies faster than a cage full of
rabbits. This contributed to Hannah's heavy heart.

Even though Peninnah bore Elkanah many children, he
still made it clear Hannah was his favorite. Talk about dysfunctional family dynamics. This made Peninnah jealous, and
she made sure Hannah paid for her unhappiness. So not only
did Hannah mourn her barren womb, she had to deal with a
petty second wife shooting ugly barbs at her. Because of this,
Hannah's self-worth remained non-existent.

In ancient times, women were primarily defined and
fulfilled by their ability to have children; they didn't

have careers or other ways to contribute to society or to create a sense of duty for themselves, as women do today.

Women in the Bible for Dummies

Though Hannah didn't understand why God didn't bless her with children, she continued to be faithful. A much-anticipated journey to the temple in Shiloh afforded Hannah a chance to pour out her heart to God through prayer. And pour out her heart she did – year after year. Hannah had no way of knowing God would eventually answer her prayers.

So often, I've thought if God didn't answer my prayer immediately, then it wouldn't be answered at all, or the answer was simply no. I've learned through the years that God's timing isn't always our timing. And if it hasn't happened yet, it doesn't mean it won't happen. Hannah learned this lesson, too.

"Why are you crying, Hannah?" Elkanah would ask. Why aren't you eating? Why be downhearted just because you have no children? You have me – isn't that better than having ten sons?"

1 Samuel 1:8

Well, let's give Elkanah an A for effort. But like most men, he didn't have a clue what his wife was feeling.

I'd say Hannah had a classic case of depression. And who wouldn't be depressed living day after day with her tormentor, Peninnah?

Though her husband tried to comfort her, he just made it worse. *You have me – isn't that better than having ten sons?"* Sounds callous, doesn't it? Hannah probably hoped he'd take her into his arms and comfort her. Didn't happen – let's just chalk it up to ignorance, because the Bible makes it clear he loved Hannah.

> *Eli the priest was sitting at his customary place beside the entrance to the Tabernacle. Hannah was in deep anguish, crying bitterly as she prayed to the Lord. And she made this vow, "Oh Lord of Heaven's Armies, if you will look upon my sorrow and answer my prayer and give me a son, then I will give him back to you. He will be yours for his entire lifetime, and as a sign that he has been dedicated to the Lord, his hair will never be cut."*
>
> *1 Samuel 1:10-11*

At the point of desperation, she went into the temple and poured out her anguish to God. We know Hannah was at the end of her rope, because she struck a bargain with God. If God gave her a son she would dedicate him to service at the temple. And Hannah would live to see that day come. But for now, she was praying her little heart out.

> *As she was praying to the Lord, Eli watched her. Seeing her lips move but hearing no sound, he thought she had been drinking. "Must you come here drunk?" he demanded. "Throw away your wine."*
>
> *"Oh no, sir!" she replied. "I haven't been drinking wine or anything stronger. But I am discouraged, and I was pouring out my heart to the Lord. Don't think I am a wicked woman! For I have been praying out of great anguish and sorrow."*
>
> *1 Samuel 1:13-16*

While she prayed, Eli, the priest, watched her. He saw her lips moving, but didn't hear any words. He assumed, which can be dangerous, that she'd been dipping in the wine and was drunk.

And he wasn't very nice about it either. He was downright angry. *"Must you come here drunk?" he demanded. "Throw away your wine"* (1 Samuel 1:14).

This is probably where I'd show my righteous indignation. How dare the priest call me drunk when I was praying to God? But Hannah chose the high road and kept her composure.

"Oh my, no! I'm not drunk. I'm pouring out my anguish to the Lord. Please don't think bad of me."

Eli back-pedaled, changing his tune. *"In that case," Eli said, "go in peace! May the God of Israel grant the request you have asked of him"* (1 Samuel 1:17).

Hannah wasn't the first woman in the Bible to long for a child while another wife bore many children. But she handled it with grace. Sarah laughed when she was told she'd have a child, Rebekah was indifferent, and Rachel threatened God with her life, "Give me children, or else I die."

> *The entire family got up early the next morning and went to worship the Lord once more. Then they returned home to Ramah. Then she went back and began to eat again, and she was no longer sad. When Elkanah slept with Hannah, the Lord remembered her plea, and in due time she gave birth to a son.*
>
> *1 Samuel 1:19-20*

When Hannah left the temple, her heart was light. She was a different woman than when she had come. Whether she had purged herself of her depression by talking to God, or gained strength from Eli's blessing, she was now confident things would change for her. And they did.

God blessed Hannah and she gave birth to a son she named Samuel, which means "asked of the Lord." Hannah kept her promise to God and after weaning Samuel; she took him to the temple to grow in stature and the knowledge of God. Nor did she wash her hands of Samuel – every year she would sew him a new coat and take it to him when they traveled to the temple.

After Eli saw Hannah's unselfishness, he asked God to bless her. She would go on to have three sons and two daughters. Remember, God's timing isn't always our timing. But it doesn't mean it won't happen. If Hannah were here today, she would tell you *her* story.

A thought to bloom by

Hannah bloomed where she was – even through challenging circumstances.

A verse to bloom by

Look at the lilies and how they grow. They don't work or make their clothing, yet Solomon in all his glory was not dressed as beautifully as they are. And if God cares so wonderfully for flowers that are here today and thrown into the fire tomorrow, he will certainly care for you. Why do you have so little faith?

Luke 12:27-28

A prayer to bloom by

Abba, thank you for all that we have. Everything good comes from you. Abba, sometimes I don't understand why my prayers aren't answered. Show me how to wait on your answers. Hannah never wavered from praying for a son even though it took many years. Please give me unwavering faith like Hannah's'. In Jesus' name, amen.

APPLICATION QUESTIONS:

- What challenging circumstances are you living in?

- Are you blooming or wilting?

- What helps you to bloom?

Research

Deen, Edith, *All of the Women of the Bible*, New York: Harper One, 1955.

New Living Translation, Chronological Life Application Study Bible, Carol Stream: Tyndale House Publishers, Inc., 2013.

Trigilio, Jr., Rev. John, and Brightenti, Rev. Kenneth, *Women in the Bible for Dummies*, Hoboken: Wiley Publishing, Inc., 2005.

CPSIA information can be obtained
at www.ICGtesting.com
Printed in the USA
FFOW05n1315261217